Coriolanus

By William Shakespeare

Edited by Rob Hastie and Josie Rourke

BLOOMSBURY
LONDON · NEW DELHI · NEW YORK · SYDNEY

Bloomsbury Methuen Drama
An imprint of Bloomsbury Publishing Plc

50 Bedford Square	1385 Broadway
London	New York
WC1B 3DP	NY 10018
UK	USA

www.bloomsbury.com

Bloomsbury is a registered trade mark of Bloomsbury Publishing Plc

This edited version of Shakespeare's play first published 2014
Reprinted 2014 (four times)

© Rob Hastie and Josie Rourke 2014

Consultant editor: Peter Holland

Donmar Warehouse have asserted their right under the Copyright,
Designs and Patents Act, 1988, to be identified as author of this work.

British Library Cataloguing-in-Publication Data
A catalogue record for this book is available from the British Library.

ISBN: PB: 978-1-4725-7677-4
ePub: 978-1-4725-7679-8
ePDF: 978-1-4725-7678-1

Library of Congress Cataloging-in-Publication Data
A catalog record for this book is available from the Library of Congress.

Typeset by Mark Heslington Ltd, Scarborough, North Yorkshire
Printed and bound in Great Britain

A note on the text

The text you find here was prepared for the production of *Coriolanus* that had its first performance at the Donmar Warehouse on 6th December 2013.

We publish the text in the hope that it may be of interest to those who saw the production, or to a reader curious about the choices we made with the play. This is not an academic edition of *Coriolanus*; nor is it a blueprint for any other production. The choices we made were for this specific company of actors, to play into the particular dynamic of the Donmar space.

In preparing this text we have been guided by an instinct that this, one of Shakespeare's longest tragedies, is also narratively one of his purest. There is no sub-plot. We have cut for length, certainly, but have also worked to translate the epic into our unique, three-sided, high-ceilinged, 251-seat theatre.

Coriolanus exists in only one original version. Unlike many of Shakespeare's plays, it was not published in his lifetime, and has survived only in the First Folio of his Complete Works, published seven years after his death, where it is sandwiched between *Troilus and Cressida* and *Titus Andronicus* in the Tragedies. Having only one version simplified our work to some extent, and we have worked from the Folio text to edit and punctuate ours.

We are indebted to Peter Holland whose guidance, both as a correspondent and in his excellent notes to the Arden edition of the play, has been invaluable. We (and perhaps our audiences) will always be grateful for his urging us to go further with some cuts and his suggestion to reinstate two lines that we had removed.

It may be worth noting that we have made an alteration to the order of scenes in Act Five, and have borrowed two lines from *Henry V* and one from *King John*.

This is my opportunity to acknowledge the scholarship and great theatrical acumen of my friend and our associate director, Rob Hastie. His abilities in the editing of

Shakespeare plays far exceed my own. Sitting at a kitchen table in the middle of rural France, hemmed in by essays on, and editions of, *Coriolanus*, we began our work on the play. It is more a testament to his great good humour than my fine Shakespearean sensibilities that it proved one of the happiest weeks of my life. It is an amazement and a relief to me that working on such a bloody play proved such good fun.

Josie Rourke
December 2013

First performed at the Donmar Warehouse on 6 December 2013. This production was broadcast live into cinemas around the world in partnership with National Theatre Live on 30 January 2014.

Cast in alphabetical order:

Valeria, Fourth Citizen, Ensemble	Jacqueline Boatswain
Cominius	Peter De Jersey
Titus Lartius	Alfred Enoch
Volumnia	Deborah Findlay
Aufidius	Hadley Fraser
Menenius	Mark Gatiss
Caius Martius Coriolanus	Tom Hiddleston
Virgilia	Birgitte Hjort Sørensen
Brutus	Elliot Levey
First Citizen, Ensemble	Rochenda Sandall
Sicinia	Helen Schlesinger
Second Citizen, Ensemble	Mark Stanley
Third Citizen, Ensemble	Dwane Walcott
Young Martius	Rudi Goodman
	Thomas Harrison
	Joe Willis

Director	Josie Rourke
Designer	Lucy Osborne
Lighting Designer	Mark Henderson
Sound Designer	Emma Laxton
Video Designer	Andrzej Goulding
Composer	Michael Bruce
Movement	Jonathan Watkins
Fight Director	Richard Ryan
Casting Director	Alastair Coomer Cdg
Children's Casting	Vicky Richardson
Production Manager	Kate West
Company Stage Manager	Sunita Hinduja
Deputy Stage Manager	Erin Murphy
Assistant Stage Manager	Sally Inch
Associate Director	Rob Hastie
Assistant Director	Oonagh Murphy
Vocal Coach	Barbara Houseman
Dialect Coach	Majella Hurley
Costume Supervisor	Ed Parry
Wigs And Make Up Supervisor	Michael Ward

Coriolanus

1.1

Enter a company of mutinous Citizens, with staves, clubs, and other weapons.

First Citizen
Before you proceed any further, hear me speak.

Second Citizen
Speak.

First Citizen
You are both resolved rather to die than to famish?

Second Citizen
Resolved.

First Citizen
First, you know Caius Martius is chief enemy to the people.

Second Citizen
We know't.

First Citizen
Let us kill him, and we'll have grain at our own price. Is't a verdict?

Third Citizen
One word, good citizen. You would proceed especially against Caius Martius?

First Citizen
Against him first. He's a very dog to the commonality.

Third Citizen
Consider you what services he has done for his country?

First Citizen
Very well, and could be content to give him good report for't, but that he pays himself with being proud.

Second Citizen
Nay, but speak not maliciously.

First Citizen

I say unto you, what he hath done famously, he did it to
that end. Though soft-conscienced men can be content to
say it was for his country, he did it to please his mother
and to be proud.

Second Citizen

What shouts are these?

First Citizen

The other side o'th'city is risen. Why stay we prating
here? To th'Capitol!

Second Citizen

Come, come!

First Citizen

Soft! who comes here?

Enter **Menenius Agrippa**.

Second Citizen

Worthy Menenius Agrippa, one that hath always loved the
people.

Menenius

What work's, my countrymen, in hand?
Where go you
With bats and clubs? The matter? Speak, I pray you.

First Citizen

Our business is not unknown to the senate. They say poor
suitors have strong breaths. They shall know we have
strong arms too.

Menenius

I tell you, friends, most charitable care
Have the patricians of you and you slander
The helms o' the state, who care for you like fathers,
When you curse them as enemies.

First Citizen

Care for us! They ne'er cared for us yet: suffer us to

famish, and their store-houses crammed with grain;
repeal daily any wholesome act established against the
rich, and provide more piercing statutes daily, to chain up
and restrain the poor.

Menenius

I shall tell you
A pretty tale: it may be you have heard it,
But since it serves my purpose I will venture
To stale't a little more.

First Citizen

Well, I'll hear it, sir: yet you must not think to fob off our
disgrace with a tale.

Menenius

There was a time when all the body's parts
Rebelled against the belly, thus accused it:
That only like a gulf it did remain
I' the midst o' the body, idle and unactive,
Still cupboarding the viand, never bearing
Like labour with the rest, where the other instruments
Did see and hear, devise, instruct, walk, feel,
And, mutually participate, did minister
Unto the appetite and affection common
Of the whole body. The belly answered –

First Citizen

Well, sir, what answer made the belly?

Menenius

Well, I shall tell you. With a kind of smile,
For look you, I may make the belly smile
As well as speak – it –

First Citizen

What?

Menenius

I will tell you.

First Citizen

You're long about it.

Menenius

Note me this, good friend:

Your most grave belly was deliberate,

Not rash like his accusers, and thus answered:

'True is it, my incorporate friends,' quoth he,

'That I receive the general food at first,

Which you do live upon; and fit it is,

Because I am the store-house and the shop

Of the whole body. But, if you do remember,

I send it through the rivers of your blood,

Even to the court, the heart, to the seat o' the brain;

And I can make my audit up that all

From me do back receive the flour of all

And leave me but the bran.' What say you to't?

First Citizen

It was an answer. How apply you this?

Menenius

The senators of Rome are this good belly,

And you the mutinous members. For examine

Their counsels and their cares, and you shall find

No public benefit which you receive

But it proceeds or comes from them to you

And no way from yourselves. What do you think?

You, the great toe of this assembly?

First Citizen

I the great toe? Why the great toe?

Menenius

For that, being one o' the lowest, basest, poorest,

Of this most wise rebellion, thou go'st foremost.

Enter **Caius Martius**.

Hail, noble Martius!

Martius

Thanks. What's the matter, you dissentious rogues,
That, rubbing the poor itch of your opinion,
Make yourselves scabs?

Second Citizen

We have ever your good word.

Martius

He that will give good words to thee will flatter
Beneath abhorring. What would you have, you curs,
That like nor peace nor war? The one affrights you,
The other makes you proud. He that trusts to you,
Where he should find you lions, finds you hares,
Where foxes, geese you are. Who deserves greatness
Deserves your hate. Hang ye! Trust Ye?
With every minute you do change a mind
And call him noble that was now your hate,
Him vile that was your garland. What's the matter?
What's their seeking?

Menenius

For corn at their own rates, whereof, they say,
The city is well stored.

Martius

Hang 'em! They say!
They'll sit by the fire, and presume to know
What's done i' the Capitol, who's like to rise,
Who thrives and who declines; side factions and give out
Conjectural marriages, making parties strong
And feebling such as stand not in their liking
Below their cobbled shoes. They say there's grain enough!
Would the nobility lay aside their ruth
And let me use my sword.

Menenius

Nay, these are almost thoroughly persuaded.
What says the other troop?

Martius

They are dissolved. Hang 'em!
They said they were a-hungry, sighed forth proverbs:
That hunger broke stone walls, that dogs must eat,
That meat was made for mouths. So with these shreds
They vented their complainings, which being answered
And a petition granted them –

Menenius

What is granted them?

Martius

Five tribunes to defend their vulgar wisdoms,
Of their own choice. One's Junius Brutus,
Sicinia Veluta, and I know not. 'Sdeath,
The rabble should have first unroofed the city,
Ere so prevailed with me. It will in time
Win upon power and throw forth greater themes
For insurrection's arguing.

Menenius

This is strange.

Martius

Go get you home, you fragments.

Enter **Cominius** *and* **Titus Lartius**, **Junius Brutus** *and*
Sicinia Velutus.

Lartius

Where's Caius Martius?

Martius

Here. What's the matter?

Cominius

Martius, 'tis true that you have lately told us;
The Volsces are in arms.

Martius

They have a leader,
Tullus Aufidius, that will put you to 't.

I sin in envying his nobility,
And were I any thing but what I am,
I would wish me only he.

Cominius

You have fought together.

Martius
Were half to half the world by the ears and he
Upon my party, I'd revolt to make
Only my wars with him. He is a lion
That I am proud to hunt.

Menenius

Then, worthy Martius,
Attend upon Cominius to these wars.

Cominius
It is your former promise.

Martius

Sir, it is,
And I am constant. Titus Lartius, thou
Shalt see me once more strike at Tullus' face.
What, art thou stiff? Stand'st out?

Lartius

No, Caius Martius.
I'll lean upon one crutch and fight with t'other
Ere stay behind this business.

Menenius

O, true-bred!

Cominius
Your company to the Capitol.

Martius

Lead you on.

Citizens steal away. Exeunt all but **Sicinia** *and* **Brutus**.

Sicinia
Was ever man so proud as is this Martius?

Brutus

He has no equal.

Sicinia

When we were chosen tribunes for the people –

Brutus

Marked you his lip and eyes?

Sicinia

Nay, but his taunts.

Brutus

Being moved, he will not spare to gird the gods.

Sicinia

Bemock the modest moon.

Brutus

The present wars devour him! He is grown
Too proud to be so valiant.

Sicinia

Such a nature,
Tickled with good success, disdains the shadow
Which he treads on at noon. Let's hence, and hear
How the dispatch is made.

Brutus

Let's along.

Exeunt.

1.2

Enter **Tullus Aufidius** *and his Lieutenant, and a Senator.*

Volscian Senator

So, your opinion is, Aufidius,
That spies of Rome have entered Volscian counsels
And know how we proceed?

Aufidius

                         Is it not yours?
What ever have been thought on in this state,
That could be brought to bodily act ere Rome
Had circumvention? 'Tis not four days gone
Since I heard thence; these are the words: you have
The letter here?

Lieutenant

Sir, here it is.

Aufidius (*Reads.*)

'They have pressed a power. The famine is great,
The people mutinous. And it is rumoured,
Cominius, Martius your old enemy,
Who is of Rome worse hated than of you,
And Titus Lartius, a most valiant Roman,
These three lead on this preparation
Whither 'tis bent. Most likely 'tis for Corioles.
Consider of it.'

Volscian Senator

                 Our army's in the field.
We never yet made doubt but Rome was ready
To answer us.

Aufidius

                 Nor did you think it folly
To keep your great pretences veiled till when
They needs must show themselves; which in the hatching,
It seemed, appeared to Rome. Beseech you sir,
Recall my power, and fortify your city.

Volscian Senator

                            Noble Aufidius,
Let us alone to guard Corioles.
If they set down before 's, for the remove
Bring your army; but, I think, you'll find
They're not prepared for us.

Aufidius

O, doubt not that;
I speak from certainties. Nay, more,
Some parcels of their power are forth already,
And only hitherward.

Volscian Senator

Recall your power.
Corioles gives you thanks, noble Aufidius.

Aufidius

The gods assist and keep your honours safe.
If we and Caius Martius chance to meet
'Tis sworn between us we shall ever strike
Till one can do no more.

Exeunt.

1.3

Enter **Volumnia**, **Virgilia** *and* **Young Martius**.

Volumnia

I pray you, daughter, sing; or express yourself in a more
comfortable sort: if my son were my husband, I should
freelier rejoice in that absence wherein he won honour
than in the embracements of his bed where he would
show most love. When yet he was but tender-bodied and
the only son of my womb, when youth with comeliness
plucked all gaze his way, when for a day of kings'
entreaties a mother should not sell him an hour from her
beholding, I, considering how honour would become
such a person, that it was no better than picture-like to
hang by the wall, if renown made it not stir, was pleased to
let him seek danger where he was like to find fame. To a
cruel war I sent him; from whence he returned, his brows
bound with oak. I tell thee, daughter, I sprang not more
in joy at first hearing he was a man-child than now in first
seeing he had proved himself a man.

Virgilia

But had he died in the business, madam; how then?

Volumnia

Then his good report should have been my son. I therein
would have found issue. Hear me profess sincerely: had I
a dozen sons, each in my love alike and none less dear
than thine and my good Martius, I had rather had eleven
die nobly for their country than one voluptuously surfeit
out of action.

Enter a **Gentlewoman**.

Gentlewoman

Madam, the Lady Valeria is come to visit you.

Virgilia

Beseech you, give me leave to retire myself.

Volumnia

Indeed, you shall not.
Methinks I hear hither your husband's drum;
See him pluck Aufidius down by the hair;
As children from a bear, the Volsces shunning him.
Methinks I see him stamp thus, and call thus:
'Come on, you cowards! You were got in fear,
Though you were born in Rome.' His bloody brow
With his mailed hand then wiping, forth he goes –

Virgilia

His bloody brow? O Jupiter, no blood!

Volumnia

Away, you fool! It more becomes a man
Than gilt his trophy. Tell Valeria,
We are fit to bid her welcome.

Exit **Gentlewoman**.

Virgilia

Heavens bless my lord from fell Aufidius!

Volumnia

He'll beat Aufidius' head below his knee
And tread upon his neck.

Enter **Valeria**, *with an Usher and* **Gentlewoman**.

Valeria

My ladies both, good day to you.

Volumnia

Sweet madam.

Virgilia

I am glad to see your ladyship.

Valeria

How do you both? You are manifest housekeepers. What
are you sewing here? A fine spot, in good faith. How does
your little son?

Virgilia

I thank your ladyship; well, good madam.

Volumnia

He had rather see the swords, and hear a drum, than look
upon his school-master.

Valeria

O' my word, the father's son. I'll swear, 'tis a very pretty
boy. O' my troth, I looked upon him o'Wednesday half an
hour together. Has such a confirmed countenance. I saw
him run after a gilded butterfly, and when he caught it, he
let it go again, and after it again, and over and over he
tumbles, and up again, catched it again. Or whether his
fall enraged him, or how 'twas, he did so set his teeth and
tear it.

Volumnia

One on's father's moods.

Valeria

Indeed, la, 'tis a noble child. Come, lay aside your
stitchery; I must have you play the idle huswife with me
this afternoon.

Virgilia
No, good madam; I will not out of doors.

Valeria
Not out of doors!

Volumnia
She shall, she shall.

Virgilia
Indeed, no, by your patience; I'll not over the threshold till my lord return from the wars.

Valeria
Fie, you confine yourself most unreasonably. Come, you must go visit the good lady that lies in.

Virgilia
I will wish her speedy strength, and visit her with my prayers; but I cannot go thither.

Volumnia
Why, I pray you?

Virgilia
'Tis not to save labour, nor that I want love.

Valeria
You would be another Penelope: yet, they say, all the yarn she spun in Ulysses' absence did but fill Ithaca full of moths. Come, you shall go with us.

Virgilia
No, good madam, pardon me; indeed, I will not forth.

Valeria
In truth, la, go with me, and I'll tell you excellent news of your husband.

Virgilia
O, good madam, there can be none yet.

Valeria

Verily, I do not jest with you; there came news from him last night.

Virgilia

Indeed, madam?

Valeria

In earnest, it's true; I heard a senator speak it. Thus it is: the Volsces have an army forth, against whom Cominius the general is gone, with one part of our Roman power. Your lord and Titus Lartius are set down before their city Corioles. They nothing doubt prevailing and to make it brief wars. This is true, on mine honour, and so, I pray, go with us.

Virgilia

Give me excuse, good madam. I will obey you in everything hereafter.

Volumnia

Let her alone, lady; as she is now, she will but disease our better mirth.

Valeria

In troth, I think she would. Fare you well, then. Come, good sweet lady. Prithee, Virgilia, turn thy solemness out o' door and go along with us.

Virgilia

No, at a word, madam; indeed, I must not. I wish you much mirth.

Valeria

Well, then, farewell.

Exeunt.

1.4

Enter, with drum and colours, **Martius**, **Titus Lartius**, *Captains and Soldiers. To them a Messenger.*

Martius
Yonder comes news.

Lartius
A wager they will yield.

Martius
My horse to yours, no.

Lartius
'Tis done.

Martius
Agreed.

Lartius
Say, will the town surrender to our general?

Messenger
This city rams its gates up 'gainst the world.

Martius
So, the good horse is mine.

Lartius
I'll buy him of you.

Martius
No, I'll nor sell nor give him. Lend you him I will
For half a hundred years.

Lartius
Ready the men.

Martius
Now Mars, I prithee, make us quick in work.
Set me directly 'gainst Aufidius.

Lartius
Ladders, ho!

The Roman army takes up positions.

Martius
  Now put your shields before your hearts and fight
  With hearts more proof than shields. Advance, my fellows!
  He that retires I'll take him for a Volsce,
  And he shall feel mine edge.

*The Romans advance towards Corioles' walls, and start to climb the
ladders.*

They are shelled from above.

The Romans retreat, leaving **Martius** *alone.*

  All the contagion of the south light on you,
  You shames of Rome! You herd of – boils and plagues
  Plaster you o'er, that you may be abhorred
  Further than seen and one infect another
  Against the wind a mile! You souls of geese
  That bear the shapes of men, how have you run
  From slaves that apes would beat! Pluto and hell!
  All hurt behind: backs red, and faces pale
  With flight and agued fear! Mend and charge home,
  Or by the fires of heaven I'll leave the foe
  And make my wars on you! Look to't. Come on!

Climbs.

  First Soldier
  Fool-hardiness; not I.

Second Soldier
  Nor I.

First Soldier
  See, they have shut him in.

Second Soldier
  To the pot, I warrant him.

Alarum continues.

Re-enter **Titus Lartius**.

Lartius
What is become of Martius?

Second Soldier
Slain, sir, doubtless.

First Soldier
He is himself alone,
To answer all the city.

Lartius
O noble fellow!
Who sensibly outdares his senseless sword,
And, when it bows, stands up. Thou art lost, Martius.
A carbuncle entire, as big as thou art,
Were not so rich a jewel. Thou wast a soldier
Even to Cato's wish, not fierce and terrible
Only in strokes; but, with thy grim looks and
The thunder-like percussion of thy sounds,
Thou madst thine enemies shake, as if the world
Were feverous and did tremble.

Enter **Cominius**.

Cominius
Where is Martius?

Lartius
Lost.
Alone he fights within Corioles.

Cominus
O Martius.
Such manhood is called foolery
Where it stands against a falling fabric
Hadst though but breathed we should have come off
Like Romans, neither foolish in our stands,
Nor cowardly in retire. Believe me sirs,
We shall be charged again.

Re-enter **Martius**, *bleeding*.

First Soldier

Look, sir.

Cominius

Who's yonder,
That does appear as he were flayed? O gods
He has the stamp of Martius, and I have
Before-time seen him thus.

Martius

So, now the gates are ope: now prove good seconds.

Cominius

Flower of warriors!

Lartius

Worthy sir, thou bleed'st.
Thy exercise hath been too violent for
A second course of fight.

Martius

Sir, praise me not;
My work hath yet not warmed me
The blood I drop is rather physical
Than dangerous to me. To Aufidius thus
I will appear and fight.

Cominius

Though I could wish
You were conducted to a gentle bath
And balms applied to you, yet dare I never
Deny your asking.

Martius

If any such be here,
As it were sin to doubt, that love this painting
Wherein you see me smeared; if any fear
Lesser his person than an ill report;
If any think brave death outweighs bad life
And that his country's dearer than himself;
Let him alone, or so many so minded,

Wave thus, to express his disposition,
And follow Martius.

*They all shout and wave their swords, take him up in their arms, and
cast up their caps.*

O, me alone! Make you a sword of me?
If these shows be not outward, which of you
But is four Volsces? None of you but is
Able to bear against the great Aufidius
A shield as hard as his.

Cominius

                    Come on, my fellows.
Make good this ostentation, and you shall
Divide in all with us.

They fight, and all enter the city.

1.5

Alarum as in battle. Enter, from opposite sides, **Martius** *and*
Aufidius.

Martius

I'll fight with none but thee, for I do hate thee
Worse than a promise-breaker.

Aufidius

                              We hate alike.
Not Afric owns a serpent I abhor
More than thy fame and envy. Fix thy foot.

Martius

Let the first budger die the other's slave,
And the gods doom him after!

Aufidius

                    If I fly, Martius,
Hollo me like a hare.

Martius

> Within these three hours, Tullus,
> Alone I fought in your Corioles' walls,
> And made what work I pleased. 'Tis not my blood
> Wherein thou seest me masked. For thy revenge
> Wrench up thy power to the highest.

Aufidius

>   Wert thou Hector
> Thou shouldst not scape me here.

They fight, and certain Volsces come to the aid of **Aufidius**.
Martius *fights till they be driven in breathless.*

> Officious, and not valiant, you have shamed me
> In your condemned seconds.

Exeunt.

1.6

*Flourish. Alarum. A retreat is sounded. Flourish. Enter, from one
side,* **Cominius** *with the Romans; from the other side,* **Martius**,
with his arm in a scarf.

Cominius

> If I should tell thee o'er this thy day's work,
> Thou'ldst not believe thy deeds. But I'll report it
> Where senators shall mingle tears with smiles,
> And where the dull tribunes, that hate thine honours,
> Shall say against their hearts 'We thank the gods
> Our Rome hath such a soldier.'

Enter **Titus Lartius**, *with his power, from the pursuit.*

Martius

> Pray now, no more. My mother,
> Who has a charter to extol her blood,
> When she does praise me grieves me. I have done
> As you have done; that's what I can; induced
> As you have been; that's for my country:

He that has but effected his good will
Hath overta'en mine act.

Cominius

You shall not be
The grave of your deserving. Rome must know
The value of her own – before our army hear me.

Martius

I have some wounds upon me, and they smart
To hear themselves remembered.

Cominius

Should they not,
Well might they fester 'gainst ingratitude,
And cure themselves with death. Of all the horses –
Whereof we have ta'en good, and good store – of all
The treasure in this field achieved and city,
We render you the tenth.

Martius

I thank you, general,
But cannot make my heart consent to take
A bribe to pay my sword. I do refuse it,
And stand upon my common part with those
That have beheld the doing.

*A long flourish. They all cry 'Martius! Martius!' cast up their caps
and lances.* **Cominius** *and* **Lartius** *stand bare.*

Martius

May these same instruments, which you profane,
Never sound more! When drums and trumpets shall
I' the field prove flatterers, let courts and cities be
Made all of false-faced soothing. No more, I say!
For that I have not washed my nose that bled,
Or foiled some feeble wretch, which without note
Here's many else have done, you shout me forth
In acclamations hyperbolical.

Cominius

    If 'gainst yourself you be incensed, we'll put you,
    Like one that means to harm himself, in manacles,
    Then reason safely with you. Therefore be it known,
    As to us, to all the world, that Caius Martius
    Wears this war's garland; and from this time forth,
    For what he did before Corioles, call him,
    With all the applause and clamour of the host,
    Caius Martius Coriolanus.
    Bear the addition nobly ever!

Flourish. Trumpets sound, and drums.

All

    Caius Martius Coriolanus!

Coriolanus

    I will go wash;
    And when my face is fair, you shall perceive
    Whether I blush or no. Howbeit, I thank you.

Cominius

                            So, to our tent,

Coriolanus

    The gods begin to mock me. I, that now
    Refused most princely gifts, am bound to beg
    Of my lord general.

Cominius

                    Take't, 'tis yours. What is't?

Coriolanus

    I sometime lay here in Corioles
    At a poor man's house. He used me kindly.
    He cried to me; I saw him taken prisoner;
    But then Aufidius was with in my view,
    And wrath o'erwhelm'd my pity. I request you
    To give my poor host freedom.

Cominius

                  O, well begged!
    Were he the butcher of my son, he should
    Be free as is the wind. Deliver him, Titus.

Lartius

Martius, his name?

Coriolanus

          By Jupiter! forgot.
I am weary; yea, my memory is tired.
Have we no wine here?

Cominius

          Go we to our tent.
The blood upon your visage dries; 'tis time
It should be looked to. Come.

Exeunt.

1.7

Enter **Tullus Aufidius**, *bloody, with his Lieutenant.*

Aufidius

The town is ta'en.

Lieutenant

'Twill be delivered back on good condition.

Aufidius

Condition!
I would I were a Roman, for I cannot,
Being a Volsce, be that I am. Condition?
What good condition can a treaty find
For th'side that is defeated? Five times, Martius,
I have fought with thee: so often hast thou beat me,
And wouldst do so, I think, should we encounter
As often as we eat. By th'elements,
If e'er again I meet him face to face,
He's mine, or I am his. Mine appetite
Hath not that honour in't it had, for where
I thought to crush him in an equal force,
True sword to sword, I'll potch at him some way.
Or wrath or craft will get him.

Lieutenant

He's the devil.

Aufidius

Bolder, though not so subtle. My valour's poisoned.
Where'er I find him, in his home, in sanctuary,
Or in the Capitol, naked, sick, asleep,
Nor prayers of priests nor time of sacrifice
Shall lift their rotten privilege against
My hate to Martius. Whereso'er, I would
Wash my fierce hand in's heart. Go you to th'city.
Learn how 'tis held, and what they are that must
Be hostages for Rome.

Lieutenant

Will not you go?

Aufidius

I am attended at the cypress grove. I pray you –
'Tis south the city mills – bring me word thither
How the world goes, that to the pace of it
I may spur on my journey.

Lieutenant

I shall, sir.

Exeunt.

2.1

Enter **Menenius** *with the two Tribunes of the people,* **Sicinia** *and* **Brutus**.

Menenius

The augurer tells me we shall have news tonight.

Brutus

Good or bad?

Menenius

Not according to the prayer of the people, for they love
not Martius.

Sicinia

Nature teaches beasts to know their friends.

Menenius

Pray you, who does the wolf love?

Sicinia

The lamb.

Menenius

Ay, to devour him; as the hungry plebeians would the
noble Martius.

Brutus

He's a lamb indeed, that baas like a bear.

Menenius

He's a bear indeed, that lives like a lamb. You two are wise
ones: tell me one thing that I shall ask you.

Both

Well, sir.

Menenius

In what enormity is Martius poor in, that you two have
not in abundance?

Brutus

He's poor in no one fault, but stored with all.

Sicinia

Especially in pride.

Brutus

And topping all others in boasting.

Menenius

This is strange now. Do you two know how you are
censured here in the city, I mean of us o' the right-hand
file? Do you?

Sicinia

How are we censured?

Brutus

Why are we censured?

Menenius

You blame Martius for being proud?

Brutus

We do it not alone, sir.

Menenius

I know you can do very little alone, for your helps are
many, or else your actions would grow wondrous single.
Your abilities are too infant-like for doing much alone.
You talk of pride. O that you could turn your eyes toward
the napes of your necks, and make but an interior survey
of your good selves! O that you could!

Brutus

What then, sir?

Menenius

Why, then you should discover a brace of unmeriting,
proud, violent, testy magistrates, alias fools, as any in
Rome.

Sicinia

Menenius, you are known well enough too.

Menenius

I am known to be a humorous patrician, and one that
loves a cup of hot wine with not a drop of allaying Tiber
in't; hasty and tinder-like upon too trivial motion; one
that converses more with the buttock of the night than
with the forehead of the morning. What I think I utter,
and spend my malice in my breath. What harm can your
blind conspectuities glean out of this character, if I be
known well enough too?

Brutus

Come, sir, come, we know you well enough.

Menenius

You know neither me, yourselves nor any thing. You are
ambitious for poor knaves' caps and legs: you wear out a
good wholesome forenoon in hearing a cause between an
orange wife and a fosset-seller; and then rejourn the
controversy of three pence to a second day of audience.
You are a pair of strange ones.

Brutus

Come, come, you are well understood to be a perfecter
giber for the table than a necessary bencher in the
Capitol.

Menenius

Good e'en to your worships. More of your conversation
would infect my brain, being the herdsmen of the beastly
plebeians. I will be bold to take my leave of you.

Brutus and **Sicinia** *go aside.*

Enter **Volumnia**, **Virgilia**, *and* **Valeria**.

How now, my as fair as noble ladies – and the moon, were
she earthly, no nobler – whither do you follow your eyes
so fast?

Volumnia

Honourable Menenius, my boy Martius approaches. For
the love of Juno, let's go.

Menenius

Ha! Martius coming home!

Volumnia and **Virgilia**

Nay, 'tis true.

Volumnia

Look, here's a letter from him. The state hath another, his
wife another, and I think there's one at home for you.

Menenius

I will make my very house reel tonight. A letter for me!

Virgilia

Yes, certain, there's a letter for you. I saw it.

Menenius

A letter for me! Is he not wounded? He was wont to come home wounded.

Virgilia

O, no, no, no.

Volumnia

O, he is wounded; I thank the gods for't.

Menenius

So do I too, if it be not too much. Brings he victory in his pocket? The wounds become him.

Volumnia

On's brows. Menenius, he comes the third time home with the oaken garland.

Menenius

Is the senate possessed of this?

Volumnia

Good ladies, let's go. Yes, yes, yes, the senate has letters from the general, wherein he gives my son the whole name of the war. He hath in this action outdone his former deeds doubly.

Menenius (*To the Tribunes.*)

God save your good worships! Martius is coming home: he has more cause to be proud. Where is he wounded?

Volumnia

I' the shoulder and i' the left arm there will be large cicatrices to show the people, when he shall stand for his place. He received in the repulse of Tarquin seven hurts i' the body.

Menenius

One i' the neck, and two i' the thigh – there's nine that I know.

Volumnia

He had, before this last expedition, twenty-five wounds
upon him.

Menenius

Now it's twenty-seven. Every gash was an enemy's grave.

A shout and flourish

Hark! the trumpets.

Volumnia

These are the ushers of Martius. Before him
He carries noise, and behind him he leaves tears.
Death, that dark spirit, in 's nervy arm doth lie,
Which being advanced, declines, and then men die.

A sennet. Trumpets sound. Enter **Cominius** *the general, and* **Titus
Lartius**; *between them* **Coriolanus**, *crowned with an oaken
garland.*

Cominius

Know, Rome, that all alone Martius did fight
Within Corioles' gates, where he hath won,
With fame, a name to Caius Martius; these
In honour follows 'Coriolanus'.
Welcome to Rome, renowned Coriolanus!

Flourish.

All

Welcome to Rome, renowned Coriolanus!

Coriolanus

No more of this, it does offend my heart.
Pray now, no more.

Cominius

                 Look, sir, your mother!

Coriolanus

                         O,
You have, I know, petition'd all the gods
For my prosperity.

Kneels.

Volumnia
                    Nay, my good soldier, up,
My gentle Martius, worthy Caius, and
By deed-achieving honour newly named –
What is it? Coriolanus must I call thee? –
But O, thy wife!

Coriolanus
                    My gracious silence, hail!
Wouldst thou have laughed had I come coffined home,
That weep'st to see me triumph? Ah, my dear,
Such eyes the widows in Corioles wear,
And mothers that lack sons.

Menenius
Now, the gods crown thee!

Coriolanus
And live you yet?

Volumnia
I know not where to turn. O, welcome home!
And welcome, general, and you're welcome all.

Menenius
A hundred thousand welcomes. I could weep
And I could laugh, I am light and heavy. Welcome.
A curse begin at very root on's heart
That is not glad to see thee!

Volumnia
                    I have lived
To see inherited my very wishes
And the buildings of my fancy. Only
There's one thing wanting, which I doubt not but
Our Rome will cast upon thee.

Coriolanus
                    Know, good mother,
I had rather be their servant in my way,
Than sway with them in theirs.

Cominius

On, to the Capitol!

Flourish. Cornets. Exeunt in state, as before. **Brutus** *and* **Sicinia**
come forward.

Brutus
All tongues speak of him, and the bleared sights
Are spectacled to see him. Such a pother
As if that whatsoever god who leads him
Were slily crept into his human powers
And gave him graceful posture.

Sicinia

On the sudden,
I warrant him consul.

Brutus

Then our office may
During his power go sleep.

Sicinia
He cannot temperately transport his honours
From where he should begin and end, but will
Lose those that he hath won.

Brutus

In that there's comfort.

Sicinia

Doubt not
The commoners for whom we stand but they
Upon their ancient malice will forget
With the least cause these his new honours, which
That he will give them make I as little question
As he is proud to do't.

Brutus

I heard him swear,
Were he to stand for consul, never would he
Appear i' the market-place nor on him put
The napless vesture of humility,

Nor showing, as the manner is, his wounds
To the people, beg their stinking breaths.

Sicinia

'Tis right.

Brutus

It was his word.

Sicinia

I wish no better
Than have him hold that purpose and to put it
In execution.

Brutus

'Tis most like he will.

Sicinia

It shall be to him then as our good wills,
A sure destruction.

Brutus

So it must fall out
To him or our authority's for an end.
We must suggest the people in what hatred
He still holds them.

Sicinia

This, as you say suggested
At some time when his soaring insolence
Shall touch the people, will be his fire
To kindle their dry stubble, and their blaze
Shall darken him for ever.

Brutus

Let's to the Capitol,
And carry with us ears and eyes for the time,
But hearts for the event.

Sicinia

Have with you.

Exeunt.

2.2

A sennet. **Cominius** *the consul,* **Menenius**, **Coriolanus**,
Senators, **Sicinia** *and* **Brutus**. *The Senators take their places; the
Tribunes take their Places by themselves.* **Coriolanus** *stands.*

Menenius
Having determined of the Volsces, it remains
As the main point of this our senate meeting
To gratify his noble service that
Hath thus stood for his country. Therefore please you
Most reverend and grave elders, to desire
The present consul, Cominius, to report
A little of that worthy work performed
By Caius Martius Coriolanus.

First Senator
Speak, good General.
Leave nothing out for length. Masters o'th'people,
We do request your kindest ears and, after,
Your loving motion toward the common body
To yield what passes here.

Sicinia
We both have hearts
Inclinable to honour and advance
The theme of our assembly.

Brutus
Which the rather
We shall be glad to do if he remember
A kinder value of the people than
He hath hereto prized them at.

Menenius
That's off. I would
You rather had been silent. He loves your people,
But tie him not to be their bedfellow.
Worthy Cominius, speak.

Coriolanus *offers to go away.*

Nay, keep your place.

First Senator

    Stay, Coriolanus.

Coriolanus

              Your honours' pardon.

    I had rather have my wounds to heal again

    Than hear say how I got them.

Brutus

            Sir, I hope

    My words disbenched you not?

Coriolanus

               No sir. Yet oft

    When blows have made me stay I fled from words.

    I'll not stay now to hear my nothings monstered.

Exit.

Menenius

    Proceed, Cominius.

Cominius

    I shall lack voice: the deeds of Coriolanus

    Should not be uttered feebly. It is held

    That valour is the chiefest virtue, and

    Most dignifies the haver. If it be,

    The man I speak of cannot in the world

    Be singly counterpoised. At sixteen years,

    When Tarquin made a head for Rome, he fought

    Beyond the mark of others. In that day's feats,

    When he might act the woman in the scene,

    He proved best man i' the field. His pupil age

    Man-entered thus, he waxed like a sea,

    And in the brunt of seventeen battles since

    He robbed all swords of the garland. For this last,

    Before and in Corioles, let me say

    I cannot speak him home. As weeds before

    A vessel under sail, so men obeyed

    And fell below his stem. His sword, death's stamp,

    Where it did mark, it took; from face to foot

He was a thing of blood, whose every motion
Was timed with dying cries. Alone he entered
The mortal gate of the city, which he painted
With shunless destiny; aidless came off,
And with a sudden reinforcement struck
Corioles like a planet; now all's his,
When by and by the din of war gan pierce
His ready sense; then straight his doubled spirit
Requickened what in flesh was fatigate,
And to the battle came he; and till we called
Both field and city ours, he never stood
To ease his breast with panting.

Menenius

                         Worthy man!

First Senator

He cannot but with measure fit the honours
Which we devise him.

Cominius

                  He covets less
Than misery itself would give, rewards
His deeds with doing them.

Menenius

                    He's right noble.
Let him be called for.

First Senator

Call Coriolanus.

Brutus

He doth appear.

Re-enter **Coriolanus**.

Menenius

The senate, Coriolanus, are well pleased
To make thee consul.

Coriolanus
                    I do owe them still
My life and services.

Menenius
                    It then remains
That you do speak to the people.

Coriolanus
                         I do beseech you,
Let me o'erleap that custom, for I cannot
Put on the gown, stand naked and entreat them
For my wounds' sake, to give their suffrage. Please you
That I may pass this doing.

Sicinia
                    Sir, the people
Must have their voices; neither will they bate
One jot of ceremony.

Coriolanus
                    It is a part
That I shall blush in acting, and might well
Be taken from the people.

Brutus
                    Mark you that?

Coriolanus
To brag unto them, thus I did, and thus,
Show them the unaching scars which I should hide,
As if I had received them for the hire
Of their breath only!

Menenius
                    Do not stand upon't.
We recommend to you, tribunes of the people,
Our purpose to them, and to our noble consul
Wish we all joy and honour.

Senators
To Coriolanus come all joy and honour!

Exeunt all but **Sicinia** *and* **Brutus**.

Brutus
You see how he intends to use the people.

Sicinia
May they perceive's intent! On th'market-place
I know they do attend us.

Exeunt.

2.3

Enter Citizens, **Brutus** *and* **Sicinia**.

First Citizen
If he do require our voices, we ought not to deny him.

Second Citizen
We may if we will.

Sicinia
I say, if he would incline to the people, there was never a
worthier man.

Enter **Coriolanus** *in a gown of humility, with* **Menenius**.

Third Citizen
Here he comes, and in the gown of humility.

Brutus
Mark his behavior.

Sicinia
You are not to stay all together, but to come by him where
he stands, by ones and twos. Every one of you has a single
honour in giving him your own voices with our own
tongues.

Third Citizen
Content, content.

Exeunt Citizens, **Sicinia** *and* **Brutus**.

Coriolanus

What must I say?
Plague upon't! I cannot bring
My tongue to such a pace. Look, sir, my wounds.
I got them in my country's service, when
Some certain of your brethren roared and ran
From the noise of our own drums.

Menenius

O me, the gods!
You must not speak of that. You must desire them
To think upon you.

Coriolanus

Think upon me? Hang 'em!
I would they would forget me.

Menenius

You'll mar all.
I'll leave you. Pray you, speak to 'em, I pray you
In wholesome manner.

Exit.

Coriolanus

Bid them wash their faces
And keep their teeth clean.

Re-enter two of the Citizens.

So, here comes a brace.
You know the cause, sirs, of my standing here.

First Citizen

We do, sir. Tell us what hath brought you to't.

Coriolanus

Mine own desert.

Second Citizen

Your own desert?

Coriolanus

Ay, but not mine own desire.

Second Citizen
How, not your own desire?

Coriolanus
No sir, 'twas never my desire yet to trouble the poor with begging.

Second Citizen
You must think, if we give you any thing, we hope to gain by you.

Coriolanus
Well then, I pray, your price o' the consulship?

First Citizen
The price is to ask it kindly.

Coriolanus
Kindly! Madam, I pray, let me have it: I have wounds to show you, which shall be yours in private. Your good voice, sir; what say you?
A match, sir. There's in all two worthy voices begged. Adieu.

Exeunt the two Citizens.

Re-enter two other Citizens.

Coriolanus
Pray you now, if it may stand with the tune of your voices that I may be consul, I have here the customary gown.

Fourth Citizen
You have deserved nobly of your country, and you have not deserved nobly.

Coriolanus
Your enigma?

Fourth Citizen
You have been a scourge to her enemies, you have been a rod to her friends; you have not indeed loved the common people.

Coriolanus

> You should account me the more virtuous that I have not
> been common in my love. I will, sir, flatter my sworn
> brother, the people, to earn a dearer estimation of them;
> 'tis a condition they account gentle. And since the wisdom
> of their choice is rather to have my hat than my heart, I
> will practice the insinuating nod and be off to them most
> counterfeitly. Therefore, beseech you, I may be consul.

Third Citizen

> You have received many wounds for your country.

Coriolanus

> I will not seal your knowledge with showing them. I will
> make much of your voices, and so trouble you no further.

Exeunt Citizens.

> Most sweet voices!
> Better it is to die, better to starve,
> Than crave the hire which first we do deserve.
> Why in this woolvish toge should I stand here
> To beg of Hob and Dick that does appear,
> Their needless vouches? Custom calls me to't.
> What custom wills, in all things should we do't,
> The dust on antique time would lie unswept
> And mountainous error be too highly heaped
> For truth to o'er-peer. Rather than fool it so,
> Let the high office and the honour go
> To one that would do thus. I am half through;
> The one part suffered, the other will I do.

Re-enter more Citizens.

> Here come more voices.
> Your voices! For your voices I have fought,
> Watched for your voices, for your voices bear
> Of wounds two dozen odd. Battles thrice six
> I have seen and heard of; for your voices have
> Done many things, some less, some more. Your voices!
> Indeed I would be consul.

All Citizens
Amen, amen. God save thee, noble consul!

Exeunt.

Coriolanus
Worthy voices!

Re-enter **Menenius**, *with* **Brutus** *and* **Sicinia**.

Menenius
You have stood your limitation, and the tribunes
Endow you with the people's voice.

Coriolanus
                                        Is this done?

Sicinia
The custom of request you have discharged.
The people do admit you, and are summoned
To meet anon, upon your approbation.

Coriolanus
Where? At the senate-house?

Sicinia
                              There, Coriolanus.

Coriolanus
May I change these garments?

Sicinia
                              You may, sir.

Coriolanus
That I'll straight do; and, knowing myself again,
Repair to the senate-house.

Menenius
I'll keep you company. Will you along?

Brutus
We stay here for the people.

Sicinia

Fare you well.

Exeunt **Coriolanus** *and* **Menenius**.

Re-enter Citizens.

Sicinia
How now, my masters! Have you chose this man?

First Citizen
He has our voices, madam.

Brutus
We pray the gods he may deserve your loves.

Fourth Citizen
Amen, sir. To my poor unworthy notice,
He mocked us when he begged our voices.

Second Citizen
Certainly, he flouted us downright.

Third Citizen
No, 'tis his kind of speech. He did not mock us.

Second Citizen
He used us scornfully. He should have showed us
His marks of merit, wounds received for's country.

Sicinia
Why, so he did, I am sure.

Third Citizen
No, no. No man saw 'em.

First Citizen
He said he had wounds, which he could show in private,
And with his hat, thus waving it in scorn,
'I would be consul,' says he. That being granted,
Here was 'I thank you for your voices. Thank you,
Your most sweet voices: now you have left your voices,
I have no further with you.' Was not this mockery?

Sicinia

> Why either were you ignorant to see't,
> Or, seeing it, of such childish friendliness
> To yield your voices?

Brutus

>   Did you not perceive
> He did solicit you in free contempt
> When he did need your loves, and do you think
> That his contempt shall not be bruising to you,
> When he hath power to crush? Why, had your bodies
> No heart among you?

Fourth Citizen

> He's not confirmed. We may deny him yet.

Second Citizen

> And will deny him:
> I'll have five hundred voices of that sound.

First Citizen

> I twice five hundred and their friends to piece 'em.

Brutus

> Get you hence instantly, and tell those friends
> They have chose a consul that will from them take
> Their liberties.

Sicinia

>   Let them assemble,
> And on a safer judgment all revoke
> Your ignorant election. Enforce his pride
> And his old hate unto you. Besides, forget not
> With what contempt he wore the humble robe,
> How in his suit he scorned you; but your loves,
> Thinking upon his services, took from you
> The apprehension of his present portance.

Brutus

>   Lay
> A fault on us, your tribunes.

Sicinia

                                   Say, you chose him
     More after our commandment than as guided
     By your own true affections. Lay the fault on us.

Brutus

     Ay, spare us not. Say we read lectures to you.
     How youngly he began to serve his country,
     How long continued, and what stock he springs of.

Sicinia

     You ne'er had done't but by our putting on.

Brutus

     Go now, and draw your number to the Capitol.

Sicinia

                                   To the Capitol, come.

Exeunt Citizens.

     We will be there before the stream o' the people;
     And this shall seem, as partly 'tis, their own,
     Which we have goaded onward.

Exeunt.

3.1

Enter **Coriolanus**, **Menenius**, **Cominius**, **Titus Lartius**, *and*
other Senators.

Cominius

     He has the peoples' voices, and the senate
     Is pleased to name him consul. Coriolanus,
     Titus Lartius is returned and brings report
     That Rome's great enemy has made new head.

Coriolanus

     So then the Volsces stand but as at first,
     Ready, when time shall prompt them, to make road
     Upon's again.

Cominius
They are worn, lord consul, so,
That we shall hardly in our ages see
Their banners wave again.

Coriolanus
                                        Saw you Aufidius?

Lartius
On safe-guard he came to me; and did curse
Against the Volsces, for they had so vilely
Yielded the town. He is retired to Antium.

Coriolanus
Spoke he of me?

Lartius
                                        He did, my lord.

Coriolanus
                                        How? what?

Lartius
How often he had met you, sword to sword;
That of all things upon the earth he hated
Your person most, that he would pawn his fortunes
To hopeless restitution, so he might
Be called your vanquisher.

Coriolanus
                                        At Antium lives he?

Lartius
At Antium.

Coriolanus
I wish I had a cause to seek him there,
To oppose his hatred fully. Welcome home.

Enter **Sicinia** *and* **Brutus**.

Behold, these are the tribunes of the people,
The tongues o' the common mouth.

Cominius
What's this?

Coriolanus
Ha! What is that?

Menenius
The matter?

Brutus
The people are incensed.

Sicinia
They cry they are at point to lose their liberties.
Martius would have all from them.

Brutus
                                        Martius,
Whom late you have named for consul.

Coriolanus
What makes this change?

Cominius
Hath he not passed the noble and the common?

Brutus
Cominius, no.

Coriolanus
                        Have I had children's voices?

Cominius
He shall to the market-place, and test it there.

Brutus
Beseech you to remain here in the senate,
It will be dangerous to go outside.

Sicinia
Remain within, or all will fall in broil.

First Senator
Tribunes, give way.

Menenius
                    Give way.

Coriolanus
                              Are these your herd?
  Must these have voices, that can yield them now
  And straight disclaim their tongues? What are your
      offices?
  You being their mouths, why rule you not their teeth?
  Have you not set them on?

Menenius
                         Be calm, be calm.

Coriolanus
  It is a purposed thing, and grows by plot
  To curb the will of the nobility.
  Suffer't, and live with such as cannot rule
  Nor ever will be ruled.

Brutus
                       Call't not a plot.
  The people cry you mocked them, and of late,
  When corn was given them gratis, you repined,
  Scandalled the suppliants for the people, called them
  Time-pleasers, flatterers, foes to nobleness.

Coriolanus
  Why, this was known before.

Brutus
                           Not to them all.

Coriolanus
  Have you informed them since?

Brutus
                            How! I inform them!

Coriolanus
  You are like to do such business.

Menenius

Let's be calm.

Cominius

The people are abused, set on. This paltering
Becomes not Rome.

Coriolanus

Tell me of corn!
This was my speech, and I will speak't again –

Menenius

Not now, not now.

First Senator

Not in this heat, sir, now.

Coriolanus

Now, as I live, I will. My nobler friends,
I crave their pardons.

First Senator

Tribunes both, give way.

Coriolanus

For the mutable, rank-scented many, let them
Regard me as I do not flatter, and
Therein behold themselves. I say again,
In soothing them, we nourish 'gainst our senate
The cockle of rebellion, insolence, sedition,
Which we ourselves have ploughed for, sowed, and
    scattered
By mingling them with us, the honoured number,
Who lack not virtue, no, nor power, but that
Which they have given to beggars.

Menenius

Well, no more.

First Senator

We thank you, no more words, pray.

Coriolanus
How? No more?
As for my country I have shed my blood,
Not fearing outward force, so shall my lungs
Coin words till their decay against those measles,
Which we disdain should tatter us, yet sought
The very way to catch them.

Brutus
                        You speak o' the people,
As if you were a god to punish.

Sicinia
                        'Twere well
We let the people know't.

Menenius
                        What, what? His choler?

Coriolanus
Choler!
Were I as patient as the midnight sleep,
By Jove, 'twould be my mind!

Sicinia
                        It is a mind
That shall remain a poison where it is,
Not poison any further.

Coriolanus
                        'Shall remain'!
Hear you this Triton of the minnows? Mark you
Her absolute 'shall'?

Cominius
                        'Twas from the canon.

Coriolanus
                                'Shall'!
O good but most unwise patricians! Why,
You grave but reckless senators, have you thus
Given Hydra here to choose an officer,
That with her peremptory 'shall,' being but

The horn and noise o' the monster's, wants not spirit
To say she'll turn your current in a ditch,
And make your channel hers? If she have power
Then vail your ignorance; if none, awake
Your dangerous lenity. If you are learned,
Be not as common fools; if you are not,
Let them have cushions by you. You are plebeians,
If they be senators. They choose their magistrate,
And such a one as she, who puts her 'shall,'
Her popular 'shall' against a graver bench
Than ever frown in Greece. By Jove himself,
It makes the consuls base, and my soul aches
To know, when two authorities are up,
Neither supreme, how soon confusion
May enter 'twixt the gap of both and take
The one by the other.

Cominius

Well, on to the market-place.

Coriolanus

Whoever gave that counsel, to give forth
The corn o' the storehouse gratis, as 'twas used
Sometime in Greece –

Menenius

Well, well, no more of that.

Coriolanus

Though there the people had more absolute power,
I say, they nourished disobedience, fed
The ruin of the state.

Brutus

Why shall the people give
One that speaks thus their voice?

Coriolanus

I'll give my reasons,
More worthier than their voices. They know the corn
Was not our recompense, resting well assured

That ne'er did service for't. Being pressed to the war,
Even when the navel of the state was touched,
They would not thread the gates. This kind of service
Did not deserve corn gratis. Being I'the war
Their mutinies and revolts, wherein they showed
Most valour, spoke not for them. The accusation
Which they have often made against the senate,
All cause unborn, could never be the motive
Of our so frank donation. Well, what then?
How shall this bosom multiplied digest
The senate's courtesy? Let deeds express
What's like to be their words: 'we did request it;
We are the greater poll, and in true fear
They gave us our demands.' Thus we debase
The nature of our seats and make the rabble
Call our cares fears, which will in time
Break ope the locks o' the senate and bring in
The crows to peck the eagles.

Menenius

                      Come, enough.

Brutus
Enough, with over-measure.

Coriolanus
                      No, take more:
What may be sworn by, both divine and human,
Seal what I end withal! This double worship,
Where one part does disdain with cause, the other
Insult without all reason; where gentry, title, wisdom,
Cannot conclude but by the yea and no
Of general ignorance – it must omit
Real necessities, and give way the while
To unstable slightness. Purpose so barred, it follows,
Nothing is done to purpose. Therefore, beseech you –
You that will be less cowardly than wise,
That love the fundamental part of state
More than you fear the change on't, and prefer

A noble life before a long, pluck out
The multitudinous tongue; let them not lick
The sweet which is their poison. Your dishonour
Mangles true judgment and bereaves the state
Of that integrity which should become't,
Not having the power to do the good it would,
For the ill which doth controlt.

Brutus

Has said enough.

Sicinia

Has spoken like a traitor, and shall answer
As traitors do.

Brutus

This a consul? No.
Let him be apprehended.

Coriolanus

Hence, you goat!

Brutus

Go, call the people, in whose name myself
Attach thee as a traitorous innovator,
An enemy of the people.

Coriolanus

Hence rotten things,
Or I shall shake thy bones out of thy garments.

Cominius

Rude sir, hands off.

Menenius

On both sides more respect.

Sicinia

Obey, we charge thee, and follow to thine answer.

Menenius

This is the way to kindle, not to quench.

First Senator
To unbuild the city and to lay all flat.

Sicinia
What is the city but the people?

Brutus
By the consent of all we were established
The people's magistrates.

Cominius
That is the way to lay the city flat,
To bring the roof to the foundation,
And bury all.

Sicinia
                    This deserves death.

Brutus
Or let us stand to our authority,
Or let us lose it. We do here pronounce,
Upon the part o' the people, in whose power
We were elected theirs, Martius is worthy
Of present death.

Sicinia
                    Therefore lay hold of him.
Bear him to the rock Tarpeian, and from thence
Into destruction cast him.

Coriolanus
                    No, I'll die here.

Drawing his sword.

There's some among you have beheld me fighting;
Come, try upon yourselves what you have seen me.

Menenius
Down with that sword! What, have you lost your wits?

Sicinia
Call the citizens!

Brutus
Lay hands upon him.

Menenius
Go, get you to your house. Be gone!

Cominius
                                        Stand fast.
We have as many friends as enemies.

Menenius
Shall it be put to that?

First Senator
                    The gods forbid!

Menenius
Tribunes, withdraw awhile.

Brutus
                    He is a viper
That would depopulate the city and
Be every man himself.

Menenius
                    Be that you seem,
Truly your country's friends and pray withdraw.
I'll undertake to bring him by and by
Where he shall answer by a lawful form.

Sicinia
We shall attend you on the market-place.

Exeunt **Sicinia** *and* **Brutus**.

Coriolanus
I would they were barbarians, as they are,
Though in Rome littered, not Romans, as they are not,
Though whelped I' the porch o' the Capitol.

Menenius
                                        Be gone!

Coriolanus
On fair ground I could beat forty of them.

First Senator
I prithee, noble friend, home to thy house.

Menenius
Leave us to cure this cause. Pray you, be gone.
I'll try whether my old wit be in request
With those that have but little.

Cominius
Will you hence?

Exeunt **Coriolanus**, **Cominius**, *and others.*

First Senator
This man has marred his fortune.

Menenius
His nature is too noble for the world.
He would not flatter Neptune for his trident,
Or Jove for's power to thunder. His heart's his mouth:
What his breast forges, that his tongue must vent,
And, being angry, does forget that ever
He heard the name of death. This must be patched
With cloth of any colour.

Exeunt.

3.2

Enter **Coriolanus** *and* **Virgilia**.

Coriolanus
I muse my mother
Does not approve me further, who was wont
To call them woollen vassals, things created
To buy and sell with groats, to show bare heads
In congregations, to yawn, be still and wonder,
When one but of my ordinance stood up
To speak of peace or war.

Enter **Volumnia**.

I talk of you.
Why did you wish me milder? Would you have me
False to my nature? Rather say I play
The man I am.

Volumnia

O, sir, sir, sir,
I would have had you put your power well on,
Before you had worn it out.

Coriolanus

Let go.

Volumnia

You might have been enough the man you are,
With striving less to be so.

Enter **Menenius**.

Menenius

Come, come, you have been too rough, something too
rough.
You must return and mend it.

Coriolanus

Let them hang.

Volumnia

Ay, and burn too.
I have a heart as little apt as yours,
But yet a brain that leads my use of anger
To better vantage.

Menenius

Well said, noble woman.

Volumnia

Pray, be counselled.

Coriolanus

What must I do?

Menenius

Return to the tribunes.

Coriolanus

Well, what then? what then?

Menenius

Repent what you have spoke.

Coriolanus

For them! I cannot do it to the gods;
Must I then do't to them?

Volumnia

You are too absolute,
Though therein you can never be too noble,
But when extremities speak. I have heard you say,
Honour and policy, like unsevered friends,
I' the war do grow together. Grant that, and tell me,
In peace what each of them by the other lose,
That they combine not there.

Coriolanus

Tush, tush!

Menenius

A good demand.

Volumnia

If it be honour in your wars to seem
The same you are not, which, for your best ends,
You adopt your policy, how is it less or worse,
That it shall hold companionship in peace
With honour, as in war, since that to both
It stands in like request?

Coriolanus

Why force you this?

Volumnia

Because that now it lies on you to speak
To the people, not by your own instruction

Nor by the matter which your heart prompts you
But with such words that are but rooted in
Your tongue, though but bastards and syllables
Of no allowance to your bosom's truth.
Now, this no more dishonours you at all
Than to take in a town with gentle words,
Which else would put you to your fortune and
The hazard of much blood.
I would dissemble with my nature where
My fortunes and my friends at stake required
I should do so in honour. I am in this,
Your wife, your son, these senators, the nobles;
And you will rather show our general louts
How you can frown than spend a fawn upon 'em
For the inheritance of their loves and safeguard
Of what that want might ruin.

Menenius

Noble lady!
Come, go with us; speak fair. You may salve so,
Not what is dangerous present, but the loss
Of what is past.

Volumnia

I prithee now, my son,
Go to them, with this bonnet in thy hand;
And thus far having stretched it – here be with them –
Thy knee bussing the stones – for in such business
Action is eloquence, and the eyes of the ignorant
More learned than the ears – bowing thy head,
As humble as the ripest mulberry
That will not hold the handling; or say to them,
Thou art their soldier, and being bred in broils
Hast not the soft way which, thou dost confess,
Were fit for thee to use as they to claim,
In asking their good loves, but thou wilt frame
Thyself, forsooth, hereafter theirs, so far
As thou hast power and person.

Menenius

This but done,
Even as she speaks, why, their hearts were yours,
For they will pardon, being asked.

Volumnia

Pray now,
Go, and be ruled, although I know thou hadst rather
Follow thine enemy in a fiery gulf
Than flatter him in a bower. Here is Cominius.

Enter **Cominius**.

Cominius

I have been i' the market-place; and, sir, 'tis fit
You make strong party, or defend yourself
By calmness or by absence. All's in anger.

Menenius

Only fair speech.

Cominius

I think 'twill serve, if he
Can thereto frame his spirit.

Volumnia

He must, and will.
Pray, say you will, and go about it.

Coriolanus

Must I
With base tongue give unto my noble heart
A lie that it must bear? Well, I will do't.
Yet, were there but this single plot to lose,
This mould of Martius, they to dust should grind it
And throw't against the wind. To the market-place!
You have put me now to such a part which never
I shall discharge to the life.

Cominius

Come, come, we'll prompt you.

Volumnia

  I prithee now, sweet son, as thou hast said
  My praises made thee first a soldier, so,
  To have my praise for this, perform a part
  Thou hast not done before.

Coriolanus

                              Well, I must do't.
  Away, my disposition, and possess me
  Some harlot's spirit! My throat of war be turned,
  Which choired with my drum, into a pipe
  Small as an eunuch, or the virgin voice
  That babies lulls asleep! The smiles of knaves
  Tent in my cheeks, and schoolboys' tears take up
  The glasses of my sight! I will not do't,
  Lest I surcease to honour mine own truth
  And by my body's action teach my mind
  A most inherent baseness.

Volumnia

                              At thy choice, then.
  To beg of thee, it is my more dishonour
  Than thou of them. Come all to ruin. Let
  Thy mother rather feel thy pride than fear
  Thy dangerous stubborness, for I mock at death
  With as big heart as thou. Do as thou list
  Thy valiantness was mine, thou suck'dst it from me,
  But owe thy pride thyself.

Coriolanus

                              Pray, be content:
  Mother, I am going to the market-place.
  Chide me no more. I'll mountebank their loves,
  Cog their hearts from them, and come home beloved
  Of all the trades in Rome. Look, I am going.
  Commend me to my wife. I'll return consul,
  Or never trust to what my tongue can do
  I' the way of flattery further.

Volumnia

Do your will.

Exit.

Cominius

Away! The tribunes do attend you. Arm yourself
To answer mildly, for they are prepared
With accusations, as I hear, more strong
Than are upon you yet.

Coriolanus

The word is 'mildly.' Pray you, let us go.
Let them accuse me by invention, I
Will answer in mine honour.

Menenius

Ay, but mildly.

Coriolanus

Well, mildly be it then. Mildly!

Exeunt.

3.3

Enter **Sicinia** *and* **Brutus**.

Brutus

In this point charge him home, that he affects
Tyrannical power. If he evade us there,
Enforce him with his envy to the people,
And that the spoil got at Corioles
Was ne'er distributed.

Enter an **AEdile**.

What, will he come?

AEdile

He's coming.

Brutus

How accompanied?

AEdile

But with Menenius, and those senators
That always favoured him.

Sicinia

Have you a catalogue
Of all the voices that we have procured
Set down by the poll?

AEdile

I have; 'tis ready.

Sicinia

Have you collected them by tribes?

AEdile

I have.

Sicinia

Assemble presently the people hither,
And when they hear me say 'It shall be so
I' the right and strength o' the commons,' be it either
For death, for fine, or banishment, then let them
If I say fine, cry 'Fine;' if death, cry 'Death.'
Insisting on the old prerogative
And power i' the truth o' the cause.

AEdile

I shall inform them.

Sicinia

Make them be strong and ready for this hint,
When we shall hap to give 't them.

Exit **AEdile**.

Brutus

Go about it.
Put him to choler straight.

Sicinia

Well, here he comes.

Enter **Coriolanus**, **Menenius**, *and* **Cominius**, *with Senators and Patricians.*

Menenius
    Calmly, I do beseech you.

Coriolanus
    The honour'd gods
    Keep Rome in safety, and the chairs of justice
    Supplied with worthy men! Plant love among 's!
    Throng our large temples with the shows of peace,
    And not our streets with war!

Cominius
    Amen, amen.

Menenius
    A noble wish.

Re-enter **AEdile**, *with Citizens.*

Sicinia
    Draw near, ye people.

AEdile
    List to your tribunes. Audience! Peace, I say!

Coriolanus
    First, hear me speak.

Both Tribunes
    Well, say. Peace, ho!

Coriolanus
    Shall I be charged no further than this present?
    Must all determine here?

Sicinia
                I do demand,
    If you submit you to the people's voices,
    Allow their officers and are content
    To suffer lawful censure for such faults
    As shall be proved upon you?

Coriolanus
I am content.

Menenius
Lo, citizens, he says he is content:
The warlike service he has done, consider. Think
Upon the wounds his body bears, which show
Like graves i' the holy churchyard.

Coriolanus
                              Scratches with briers,
Scars to move laughter only.

Menenius
                    Consider further,
That when he speaks not like a citizen,
You find him like a soldier: do not take
His rougher accents for malicious sounds –

Cominius
Well, well, no more, no more.

Coriolanus
                    What is the matter
That being passed for consul with full voice,
I am so dishonoured that the very hour
You take it off again?

Sicinia
                    Answer to us.

Coriolanus
Say, then. 'Tis true, I ought so.

Sicinia
We charge you, that you have contrived to take
From Rome all seasoned office and to wind
Yourself into a power tyrannical,
For which you are a traitor to the people.

Coriolanus
How! 'Traitor?'

Menenius

Nay, temperately! Your promise.

Coriolanus

The fires i' the lowest hell fold-in the people!
Call me their traitor! Thou injurious tribune!
Should twenty thousand deaths sit in thine eyes,
As many millions clutched within thy hands,
I'd say 'thou liest' with a voice as free
As I do pray the gods.

Sicinia

Mark you this, people?

First Citizen

To the rock, to the rock with him!

Sicinia

Peace!
We need not put new matter to his charge.
What you have seen him do and heard him speak,
Beating your officers, cursing yourselves,
Opposing laws with strokes and here defying
Those whose great power must try him; even this,
So criminal and in such capital kind,
Deserves the extremest death.

Brutus

But since he hath
Served well for Rome –

Coriolanus

What do you prate of service?

Brutus

I talk as one that knows it.

Coriolanus

You?

Menenius

Is this the promise that you made your mother?

Cominius
> Know, I pray you –

Coriolanus
>   I know no further.
> Let them pronounce the steep Tarpeian death,
> Vagabond exile, raying, pent to linger
> But with a grain a day, I would not buy
> Their mercy at the price of one fair word,
> Nor check my courage for what they can give,
> To have't with saying 'Good morrow.'

Sicinia
>   For that he has,
> As much as in him lies, from time to time
> Envied against the people, seeking means
> To pluck away their power, in the name o' the people
> And in the power of us the tribunes, we,
> Even from this instant, banish him our city,
> In peril of precipitation
> From off the rock Tarpeian never more
> To enter our Rome gates: i' the people's name,
> I say it shall be so.

Citizens
> It shall be so, it shall be so!

Cominius
> Hear me, my masters, and my common friends –

Sicinia
> He's sentenced. No more hearing.

Cominius
>   Let me speak:
> I have been consul, and can show for Rome
> Her enemies' marks upon me. I do love
> My country's good with a respect more tender,
> More holy and profound, than mine own life,
> My dear wife's estimate, her womb's increase,
> And treasure of my loins; then if I would
> Speak that –

Brutus

There's no more to be said, but he is banished,
As enemy to the people and his country:
It shall be so.

Citizens

It shall be so, it shall be so.

Coriolanus

You common cry of curs, whose breath I hate
As reek o' the rotten fens, whose loves I prize
As the dead carcasses of unburied men
That do corrupt my air, I banish you.
And here remain with your uncertainty:
Let every feeble rumour shake your hearts;
Your enemies, with nodding of their plumes,
Fan you into despair! Have the power still
To banish your defenders, till at length
Your ignorance – which finds not till it feels,
Making not reservation of yourselves,
Still your own foes – deliver you as most
Abated captives to some nation
That won you without blows! Despising,
For you, the city, thus I turn my back:
There is a world elsewhere.

Exeunt.

4.1

Enter **Coriolanus**, **Volumnia**, **Virgilia**, **Menenius**, **Cominius**,
with the young Nobility of Rome.

Coriolanus

Come, leave your tears: a brief farewell: the beast
With many heads butts me away. Nay, mother,
Where is your ancient courage? you were used
To say extremity was the trier of spirits;
That common chances common men could bear;

That when the sea was calm all boats alike
Showed mastership in floating.

Virgilia
O heavens! O heavens!

Coriolanus
                              Nay! prithee, woman –

Volumnia
Now the red pestilence strike all trades in Rome,
And occupations perish!

Coriolanus
                              What, what, what!
I shall be loved when I am lack'd. Nay, mother.
Resume that spirit, when you were wont to say,
If you had been the wife of Hercules,
Six of his labours you'd have done, and saved
Your husband so much sweat. Menenius,
Droop not; adieu. Farewell, my wife, my mother:
I'll do well yet. My sometime general,
I have seen thee stern, and thou hast oft beheld
Heart-hardening spectacles; tell these sad women
'Tis fond to wail inevitable strokes,
As 'tis to laugh at 'em. My mother, you wot well
My hazards still have been your solace and –
Believe't not lightly – though I go alone,
Like to a lonely dragon, that his fen
Makes feared and talked of more than seen – your son
Will or exceed the common or be caught
With cautelous baits and practise.

Volumnia
                              My first son.
Whither wilt thou go? Take good Cominius
With thee awhile.

Coriolanus
O the gods!

Cominius

    I'll follow thee a month, devise with thee
    Where thou shalt rest, that thou mayst hear of us
    And we of thee: so if the time thrust forth
    A cause for thy repeal, we shall not send
    O'er the vast world to seek a single man.

Coriolanus

    Fare ye well:
    Thou hast years upon thee; and thou art too full
    Of the wars' surfeits, to go rove with one
    That's yet unbruised; bring me but out at gate.
    Come, my sweet wife, my dearest mother, and
    My friends of noble touch, when I am forth,
    Bid me farewell, and smile. I pray you, come.
    While I remain above the ground, you shall
    Hear from me still, and never of me aught
    But what is like me formerly.

Menenius

                That's worthily
    As any ear can hear. Come, let's not weep.

Coriolanus

    Give me thy hand: Come.

Exeunt.

4.2

Enter **Sicinia** *and* **Brutus**.

Sicinia

    Go, see him out at gates, and follow him,
    As he hath followed you, with all despite.
    Give him deserved vexation. Let a guard
    Attend us through the city.
    He's gone, and we'll no further.
    The nobility are vexed, whom we see have sided
    In his behalf.

Brutus

Now we have shown our power,
Let us seem humbler after it is done
Than when it was a-doing.

Sicinia

                              Bid them home.
Say their great enemy is gone, and they
Stand in their ancient strength.

Brutus

Here comes his mother.

Sicinia

Let's not meet her.

Brutus

Why?

Sicinia

They say she's mad.

Brutus

They have ta'en note of us. Keep on your way.

Enter **Volumnia**, **Virgilia**, *and* **Menenius**.

Volumnia

O, ye're well met. The hoarded plague o' the gods
Requite your love!

Menenius

                    Peace, peace. Be not so loud.

Volumnia

If that I could for weeping, you should hear –
Nay, and you shall hear some. Will you be gone?

Virgilia

You shall stay too: I would I had the power
To say so to my husband.

Sicinia

                    Are you mankind?

Volumnia
Ay, fool, is that a shame? Note but this fool.
Was not a man my father? Hadst thou foxship
To banish him that struck more blows for Rome
Than thou hast spoken words?

Sicinia
O blessed heavens!

Volumnia
More noble blows than ever thou wise words,
And for Rome's good. I'll tell thee what – yet go.
Nay, but thou shalt stay too. I would my son
Were in Arabia, and thy tribe before him,
His good sword in his hand.

Sicinia
What then?

Virgilia
What then!
He'd make an end of thy posterity.

Volumnia
Bastards and all.
Good man, the wounds that he does bear for Rome!

Menenius
Come, come, peace.

Sicinia
I would he had continued to his country
As he began, and not unknit himself
The noble knot he made.

Brutus
I would he had.

Volumnia
'I would he had'! 'Twas you incensed the rabble.

Brutus
Pray, let us go.

Volumnia

Now, pray, sir, get you gone.
You have done a brave deed. Ere you go, hear this:
As far as doth the Capitol exceed
The meanest house in Rome, so far my son –
This lady's husband here, this, do you see –
Whom you have banished, does exceed you all.

Brutus

Well, well, we'll leave you.

Sicinia

Why stay we to be baited
With one that wants her wits?

Exeunt Tribunes.

Volumnia

Take my prayers with you.
I would the gods had nothing else to do
But to confirm my curses! Could I meet 'em
But once a-day, it would unclog my heart
Of what lies heavy to't.

Menenius

You have told them home;
And, by my troth, you have cause. You'll sup with me?

Volumnia

Anger's my meat; I sup upon myself,
And so shall starve with feeding. Come, let's go.
Leave this faint puling and lament as I do,
In anger, Juno-like. Come, come, come.

Menenius

Fie, fie, fie!

Exeunt.

4.3

Enter **Coriolanus** *in mean apparel, disguised and muffled.*

Coriolanus
 A goodly city is this Antium. City,
 'Tis I that made thy widows. Many an heir
 Of these fair edifices 'fore my wars
 Have I heard groan and drop. Then know me not,
 Lest that thy wives with spits and boys with stones
 In puny battle slay me.

Enter a Citizen.

                              Save you, sir.

Citizen
 And you.

Coriolanus
                    Direct me, if it be your will,
 Where great Aufidius lies. Is he in Antium?

Citizen
 He is, and feasts the nobles of the state
 At his house this night.

Coriolanus
                              Which is his house, beseech you?

Citizen
 This, here before you.

Coriolanus
 Thank you, sir. Farewell.

Exit Citizen.

 O world, thy slippery turns! Friends now fast sworn,
 Whose double bosoms seem to wear one heart,
 Whose house, whose bed, whose meal, and exercise,
 Are still together, who twin, as 'twere, in love
 Unseparable, shall within this hour,
 On a dissension of a doit, break out

To bitterest enmity. So, fellest foes,
Whose passions and whose plots have broke their sleep,
To take the one the other, by some chance,
Some trick not worth an egg, shall grow dear friends
And interjoin their issues. So with me.
My birth-place hate I, and my love's upon
This enemy town. I'll enter. If he slay me,
He does fair justice; if he give me way,
I'll do his country service.

Exit.

4.4

Enter a **Servingman**.

First Servingman
Wine, wine, wine! What service is here! I think our fellows
are asleep.

Exit.

Enter a second **Servingman**.

Second Servingman
Where's Cotus? My master calls for him. Cotus!

Exit.

Enter **Coriolanus**.

Coriolanus
A goodly house. The feast smells well, but I
Appear not like a guest.

Re-enter the first **Servingman**.

First Servingman
What would you have, friend? Whence are you?
Here's no place for you. Pray, go to the door.

Exit.

Coriolanus

I have deserved no better entertainment,
In being Coriolanus.

Re-enter second **Servingman**.

Second Servingman

Whence are you, sir? Has the porter his eyes in his head;
that he gives entrance to such companions? Pray, get you
out.

Coriolanus

Away!

Second Servingman

Away! Get you away.

Coriolanus

Now thou'rt troublesome.

Second Servingman

Are you so brave? I'll have you talked with anon.

Enter a third **Servingman**. *The first meets him.*

Third Servingman

What fellow's this?

First Servingman

A strange one as ever I looked on. I cannot get him out of
the house. Prithee, call my master to him.

Retires.

Third Servingman

What have you to do here, fellow? Pray you, avoid the
house.

Coriolanus

Let me but stand. I will not hurt your hearth.

Third Servingman

What are you?

Coriolanus
A gentleman.

Third Servingman
A marvellous poor one.

Coriolanus
True, so I am.

Third Servingman
Pray you, poor gentleman, take up some other station.
Here's no place for you. Pray you, avoid. Come.

Coriolanus
Follow your function, go, and batten on cold bits.

Pushes him away.

Third Servingman
What, you will not? Prithee, tell my master what a strange
guest he has here.

Second Servingman
And I shall.

Exit.

Third Servingman
Where dwellest thou?

Coriolanus
Under the canopy.

Third Servingman
Under the canopy!

Coriolanus
Ay.

Third Servingman
Where's that?

Coriolanus
I' the city of kites and crows.

Third Servingman

I' the city of kites and crows! What an ass it is! Then thou
dwellest with daws too?

Coriolanus

No, I serve not thy master.

Third Servingman

How, sir! Do you meddle with my master?

Coriolanus

Ay; 'tis an honester service than to meddle with thy
mistress. Thou pratest, and pratest. Serve with thy
trencher, hence!

Beats him away. Exit third **Servingman**.

Enter **Aufidius** *with the second* **Servingman**.

Aufidius

Where is this fellow?

Second Servingman

Here, sir. I'd have beaten him like a dog, but for
disturbing the lords within.

Retires.

Aufidius

Whence comest thou? What wouldst thou? Thy name?
Why speak'st not? Speak, man. What's thy name?

Coriolanus (*Unmuffling.*)

If, Tullus,

Not yet thou knowest me, and, seeing me, dost not
Think me for the man I am, necessity
Commands me name myself.

Aufidius

What is thy name?

Coriolanus

A name unmusical to the Volscians' ears,
And harsh in sound to thine.

Aufidius

                                    Say, what's thy name?
Thou hast a grim appearance, and thy face
Bears a command in't. Though thy tackle's torn,
Thou show'st a noble vessel. What's thy name?

Coriolanus

Prepare thy brow to frown. Know'st thou me yet?

Aufidius

I know thee not. Thy name?

Coriolanus

My name is Caius Martius, who hath done
To thee particularly and to all the Volsces
Great hurt and mischief; thereto witness may
My surname, Coriolanus. The painful service,
The extreme dangers and the drops of blood
Shed for my thankless country are requited
But with that surname – a good memory,
And witness of the malice and displeasure
Which thou shouldst bear me. Only that name remains.
The cruelty and envy of the people,
Permitted by our dastard nobles, who
Have all forsook me, hath devoured the rest
And suffered me by the voice of slaves to be
Whooped out of Rome. Now this extremity
Hath brought me to thy hearth; not out of hope –
Mistake me not – to save my life, for if
I had feared death, of all the men i' the world
I would have 'voided thee, but in mere spite,
To be full quit of those my banishers,
Stand I before thee here. Then if thou hast
A heart of wreak in thee, that wilt revenge
Thine own particular wrongs and stop those maims
Of shame seen through thy country, speed thee straight,
And make my misery serve thy turn. So use it
That my revengeful services may prove
As benefits to thee, for I will fight

Against my cankered country with the spleen
Of all the under fiends. But if so be
Thou darest not this and that to prove more fortunes
Thou'rt tired, then, in a word, I also am
Longer to live most weary, and present
My throat to thee and to thy ancient malice,
Which not to cut would show thee but a fool,
Since I have ever followed thee with hate,
Drawn tuns of blood out of thy country's breast,
And cannot live but to thy shame, unless
It be to do thee service.

Aufidius
                              O Martius, Martius!
Each word thou hast spoke hath weeded from my heart
A root of ancient envy. If Jupiter
Should from yond cloud speak divine things,
And say ''Tis true,' I'd not believe them more
Than thee, all noble Martius. Let me twine
Mine arms about that body, where against
My grained ash an hundred times hath broke
And scarred the moon with splinters. Here I clip
The anvil of my sword, and do contest
As hotly and as nobly with thy love
As ever in ambitious strength I did
Contend against thy valour. Know thou first,
I loved the maid I married, never man
Sigh'd truer breath. But that I see thee here,
Thou noble thing, more dances my rapt heart
Than when I first my wedded mistress saw
Bestride my threshold. Why, thou Mars! I tell thee,
We have a power on foot, and I had purpose
Once more to hew thy target from thy brawn,
Or lose mine arm for't. Thou hast beat me out
Twelve several times, and I have nightly since
Dreamt of encounters 'twixt thyself and me;
We have been down together in my sleep,
Unbuckling helms, fisting each other's throat,

And waked half dead with nothing. Worthy Martius,
Had we no quarrel else to Rome, but that
Thou art thence banished, we would muster all
From twelve to seventy, and pouring war
Into the bowels of ungrateful Rome,
Like a bold flood o'er-bear. O, come, go in,
And take our friendly senators by the hands,
Who now are here, taking their leaves of me,
Who am prepared against your territories,
Though not for Rome itself.

Coriolanus

                            You bless me, gods!

Aufidius

Therefore, most absolute sir, if thou wilt have
The leading of thine own revenges, take
The one half of my commission; and set down
As best thou art experienced, since thou know'st
Thy country's strength and weakness, thine own ways,
Whether to knock against the gates of Rome,
Or rudely visit them in parts remote,
To fright them, ere destroy. But come in,
Let me commend thee first to those that shall
Say yea to thy desires. A thousand welcomes!
And more a friend than e'er an enemy;
Yet, Martius, that was much. Your hand. Most welcome!

Exeunt.

4.5

Enter **Sicinia** *and* **Brutus**.

Sicinia

We hear not of him, neither need we fear him.

Brutus

We stood to't in good time. Is this Menenius?

Enter **Menenius**.

Sicinia
  'Tis he, 'tis he. O, he is grown most kind of late.

Both Tribunes
  Hail sir!

Menenius
              Hail to you both!

Sicinia
                    Your Coriolanus
  Is not much missed, but with his friends.
  The commonwealth doth stand, and so would do,
  Were he more angry at it.

Menenius
  All's well, and might have been much better, if
  He could have temporized.

Sicinia
                    Where is he, hear you?

Menenius
  Nay, I hear nothing. His mother and his wife
  Hear nothing from him.

Enter three or four Citizens.

First Citizen
  The gods preserve you both!

Sicinia
                    Good e'en, our neighbours.

Brutus
  Good e'en to you all, good e'en to you all.

First Citizen
  Ourselves, our wives, and children, on our knees,
  Are bound to pray for you both.

Sicinia

Live, and thrive!

Brutus

Farewell, kind neighbours. We wished Coriolanus
Had loved you as we did.

Citizens

Now the gods keep you!

Both Tribunes

Farewell, farewell.

Exeunt Citizens.

Sicinia

This is a happier and more comely time
Than when these fellows ran about the streets,
Crying confusion.

Brutus

Rome sits safe and still.

Enter **Messenger 1**.

Messenger 1

Worthy tribunes,
There is a slave, whom we have put in prison,
Reports, the Volsces with two several powers
Are entered in the Roman territories,
And with the deepest malice of the war
Destroy what lies before 'em.

Menenius

'Tis Aufidius,
Who, hearing of our Martius' banishment,
Thrusts forth his horns again into the world.

Sicinia

Come, what talk you
Of Martius?

Brutus

Go see this rumourer whipped. It cannot be
The Volsces dare break with us.

Menenius

Cannot be!
We have record that very well it can,
And three examples of the like have been
Within my age. But reason with the fellow,
Before you punish him, where he heard this,
Lest you shall chance to whip your information
And beat the messenger who bids beware
Of what is to be dreaded.

Sicinia

Tell not me.
I know this cannot be.

Brutus

Not possible.

Enter **Titus Lartius**.

Lartius

Menenius, we are sent for to the senate.
The nobles in great earnestness are going
All to the Capitol. Some news is come
That turns their countenances.

Sicinia

'Tis this slave.
Go whip him, 'fore the people's eyes.

Lartius

No, sure
The slave's report is seconded. And more,
More fearful, is delivered.

Sicinia

What more fearful?

Lartius

It is spoke freely out of many mouths –
How probable I do not know – that Martius,
Joined with Aufidius, leads a power 'gainst Rome,
And vows revenge as spacious as between
The young'st and oldest thing.

Sicinia

This is most likely!

Brutus

Raised only, that the weaker sort may wish
Good Martius home again.

Sicinia

The very trick on't.

Menenius

This is unlikely.
He and Aufidius can no more atone
Than violentest contrariety.

Enter **Cominius**.

Cominius

O, you have made good work!

Menenius

What news? What news?

Cominius

O you have helped to ravish your own daughters,
To melt the city leads upon your pates,
To see your wives dishonoured to your noses –

Menenius

Pray, your news? You have made fair work, I fear me –
If Martius should be joined with Volscians –

Cominius

If!

He is their god. He leads them like a thing
Made by some other deity than nature,

That shapes man better, and they follow him,
Against us brats, with no less confidence
Than boys pursuing summer butterflies,
Or butchers killing flies.

Menenius
                              You have made good work,
You and your apron-men, you that stood so up much
Upon the voice of occupation and
The breath of garlic-eaters!

Cominius
                              He will shake
Your Rome about your ears.

Menenius
                              You have made fair work.

Brutus
But is this true, sir?

Cominius
                    Ay, and you'll look pale
Before you find it other. He is now
Camped at Corioles, and all the regions
Do smilingly revolt; those who resist
Are mocked for valiant ignorance,
And perish constant fools. Who is't can blame him?
Your enemies and his find something in him.

Menenius
We are all undone, unless
The noble man have mercy.

Cominius
                              Who shall ask it?
The tribunes cannot do't for shame; the people
Deserve such pity of him as the wolf
Does of the shepherds. For his best friends, how may
They say 'Be good to Rome'; they charged him even
As those should do that had deserved his hate,
And therein showed like enemies.

Menenius

'Tis true.
If he were putting to my house the brand
That should consume it, I have not the face
To say 'Beseech you, cease.' You have made fair hands,
You and your crafts! You have crafted fair!

Cominius

You have brought
A trembling upon Rome, such as was never
So incapable of help.

Both Tribunes

Say not we brought it.

Menenius

How! Was it we? We loved him but, like beasts
And cowardly nobles, gave way unto your clusters,
Who did hoot him out o' the city.

Cominius

But I fear
They'll roar him in again. Tullus Aufidius,
The second name of men, obeys his points
As if he were his officer. Desperation
Is all the policy, strength and defence,
That Rome can make against them.

Enter a troop of Citizens.

Menenius

Here come the clusters.
And is Aufidius with him? You are they
That made the air unwholesome, when you cast
Your stinking greasy caps in hooting at
Coriolanus' exile. Now he's coming,
And not a hair upon a soldier's head
Which will not prove a whip. As many heads
As you threw caps up will he tumble down,
And pay you for your voices. 'Tis no matter;
If he could burn us all into one coal,
We have deserved it.

First Citizen
Faith, we hear fearful news.

Second Citizen
                           For mine own part,
When I said, banish him, I said 'twas pity.

Third Citizen
And so did I.

Fourth Citizen
And so did I, and, to say the truth, so did very many of us.
That we did, we did for the best, and though we willingly
consented to his banishment, yet it was against our will.

Cominius
You're goodly things, you voices!

Menenius
                            You have made
Good work, you and your cry! Shall's to the Capitol?

Cominius
O, ay, what else?

Exeunt **Cominius** *and* **Menenius**.

Sicinia
Go, masters, get you home. Be not dismayed.
These are a side that would be glad to have
This true which they so seem to fear. Go home,
And show no sign of fear.

First Citizen
The gods be good to us! Come, masters, let's home. I said
we were i' the wrong when we banished him.

Second Citizen
So did we all. But, come, let's home.

Exeunt Citizens

Brutus
I do not like this news.

Sicinia
  Nor I.

Brutus
  Let's to the Capitol. Would half my wealth
  Would buy this for a lie!

Sicinia
                                    Pray, let us go.

Exeunt.

4.6

Enter **Aufidius** *and his* **Lieutenant**.

Aufidius
  Do they still fly to the Roman?

Lieutenant
  I do not know what witchcraft's in him, but
  Your soldiers use him as the grace 'fore meat,
  Their talk at table, and their thanks at end,
  And you are darkened in this action, sir,
  Even by your own.

Aufidius
                    I cannot help it now,
  Unless, by trickery, I lame the foot
  Of our design. He bears himself more proudlier,
  Even to my person, than I thought he would
  When first I did embrace him. Yet his nature
  In that's no changeling, and I must excuse
  What cannot be amended.

Lieutenant
                    Yet I wish, sir –
  I mean for your particular – you had not
  Joined in commission with him, but either
  Had borne the action of yourself, or else
  To him had left it solely.

Aufidius

I understand thee well; and be thou sure,
When he shall come to his account, he knows not
What I can urge against him. Although it seems,
And so he thinks, and is no less apparent
To the vulgar eye, that he bears all things fairly.
And shows good husbandry for the Volscian state,
Fights dragon-like, and does achieve as soon
As draw his sword, yet he hath left undone
That which shall break his neck or hazard mine,
Whene'er we come to our account.

Lieutenant

Sir, I beseech you, think you he'll carry Rome?

Aufidius

All places yield to him ere he sits down.
The senators and patricians love him;
The tribunes are no soldiers, and their people
Will be as rash in the repeal, as hasty
To expel him thence. I think he'll be to Rome
As is the osprey to the fish, who takes it
By sovereignty of nature. First he was
A noble servant to them, but he could not
Carry his honours even. Whether 'twas pride,
Whether defect of judgement, or whether nature,
(Commanding peace as he controlled the war),
Or whether spices of them all have made him feared,
He's hated, and is banished. But he has a merit
To choke it in the utterance.
One fire drives out one fire; one nail, one nail;
Rights by rights falter, strengths by strengths do fail.
Come, let's away. When, Caius, Rome is thine,
Thou art poor'st of all; then shortly art thou mine.

Exeunt.

5.1

Enter **Menenius**, **Cominius**, **Sicinia**, **Brutus**, *and others.*

Menenius

No, I'll not go: you hear what he hath said
To him which was his general, who loved him
In a most dear particular. He call'd me father;
But what o' that? Go, you that banish'd him;
A mile before his tent fall down, and knee
The way into his mercy. Nay, if he coyed
To hear Cominius speak, I'll keep at home.

Cominius

He would not seem to know me.

Menenius

Do you hear?

Cominius

Yet one time he did call me by my name.
I urged our old acquaintance, and the drops
That we have bled together. Coriolanus
He would not answer to; forbade all names.
He was a kind of nothing, titleless,
Till he had forged himself a name o' the fire
Of burning Rome.

Menenius

Why, so, you have made good work!

Cominius

I minded him how royal 'twas to pardon
When it was less expected. He replied,
It was a poor petition of a state
To one whom they had punished.

Menenius

Very well.

Could he say less?

Cominius

I offered to awaken his regard
For's private friends. His answer to me was,
He could not stay to pick them from a pile
Of noisome musty chaff. He said 'twas folly,
For one poor grain or two, to leave unburnt,
And still to nose the offence.

Menenius

For one poor grain or two!
I am one of those; his mother, wife, his child,
And this brave fellow too, we are the grains.
You are the musty chaff, and you are smelt
Above the moon. We must be burnt for you.

Sicinia

Nay, pray, be patient. If you refuse your aid
In this so never-needed help, yet do not
Upbraid's with our distress. But, sure, if you
Would be your country's pleader, your good tongue,
More than the instant army we can make,
Might stop our countryman.

Menenius

                No, I'll not meddle.

Sicinia

Pray you, go to him.

Menenius

              What should I do?

Brutus

Only make trial what your love can do
For Rome, towards Martius.

Menenius

Well, and say that Martius return me,
As Cominius is returned, unheard; what then?
But as a discontented friend, grief-shot
With his unkindness? Say't be so?

Sicinia

Then take Rome's thanks,
As you intended well.

Menenius

I'll undertake 't.
I think he'll hear me. Yet, to bite his lip
And hum at good Cominius, much unhearts me.
He was not taken well; he had not dined.
The veins unfilled, our blood is cold, and then
We pout upon the morning, are unapt
To give or to forgive; but when we have stuffed
These and these conveyances of our blood
With wine and feeding, we have suppler souls
Than in our priest-like fasts. Therefore I'll watch him
Till he be dieted to my request,
And then I'll set upon him.

Brutus

You know the very road into his kindness,
And cannot lose your way.

Menenius

Good faith, I'll prove him,
Speed how it will. I shall ere long have knowledge
Of my success.

Exit.

Cominius

He'll never hear him.

Sicinia

Not?

Cominius

I tell you, he does sit in gold, his eye
Red as 'twould burn Rome, and his injury
The gaoler to his pity. I kneeled before him;
'Twas very faintly he said 'Rise;' dismissed me
Thus, with his speechless hand. What he would do,
He sent in writing after me; what he would not,

Bound with an oath to yield to his conditions.
So that all hope is vain.
Unless his noble mother, and his wife,
Who, as I hear, mean to solicit him
For mercy to his country. Therefore, let's hence,
And with our fair entreaties haste them on.

Exeunt.

5.2

Two Sentinels on guard. Enter to them, **Menenius**.

First Sentinel
Stay. Whence are you?

Second Sentinel
Stand, and go back.

Menenius
You guard like men; 'tis well. But, by your leave,
I am an officer of state, and come
To speak with Coriolanus.

First Sentinel
From whence?

Menenius
From Rome.

First Sentinel
You may not pass, you must return. Our general
Will no more hear from thence.

Second Sentinel
You'll see your Rome embraced with fire before
You'll speak with Coriolanus.

Menenius
                    Good my friends,
If you have heard your general talk of Rome,
And of his friends there, it is lots to blanks,
My name hath touched your ears; it is Menenius.

First Sentinel

Be it so; go back. The virtue of your name
Is not here passable.

Menenius

                              I tell thee, fellow,
The general is my lover. I have been
The book of his good acts, whence men have read
His name unparalleled, haply amplified;
For I have ever verified my friends,
Of whom he's chief, with all the size that verity
Would without lapsing suffer. Nay, sometimes,
Like to a bowl upon a subtle ground,
I have tumbled past the throw and in his praise
Have almost stamp'd the leasing. Therefore, fellow,
I must have leave to pass.

First Sentinel

Faith, sir, if you had told as many lies in his behalf as you
have uttered words in your own, you should not pass
here, no, though it were as virtuous to lie as to live
chastely. Therefore, go back.

Menenius

Prithee, fellow, remember my name is Menenius, always
factionary on the party of your general.

Second Sentinel

Howsoever you have been his liar, as you say you have, I
am one that, telling true under him, must say, you cannot
pass. Therefore, go back.

Menenius

Has he dined, canst thou tell? For I would not speak with
him till after dinner.

First Sentinel

You are a Roman, are you?

Menenius

I am, as thy general is.

First Sentinel

Then you should hate Rome, as he does. Can you, when
you have pushed out your gates the very defender of
them, and, in a violent popular ignorance, given your
enemy your shield, think to front his revenges with the
easy groans of old women or the palsied intercession of
such a decayed dotant as you seem to be? Can you think
to blow out the intended fire your city is ready to flame in,
with such weak breath as this? No, you are deceived;
therefore, back to Rome, and prepare for your execution.
You are condemned, our general has sworn you out of
reprieve and pardon.

Menenius

Sirrah, if thy captain knew I were here, he would use me
with estimation.

Second Sentinel

Come, my captain knows you not.

Menenius

I mean, thy general.

First Sentinel

My general cares not for you. Back, I say, go, lest I let
forth your half-pint of blood. Back, that's the utmost of
your having: back.

Menenius

Nay, but, fellow, fellow –

Enter **Coriolanus** *and* **Aufidius**.

Coriolanus

What's the matter?

Menenius

Now, you companion, you shall know now that I am in
estimation. You shall perceive that a Jack guardant cannot
office me from my son Coriolanus. Guess, but by my
entertainment with him, if thou standest not i' the state of
hanging, and swoon for what's to come upon thee.

To **Coriolanus**.

> The glorious gods sit in hourly synod about thy particular
> prosperity, and love thee no worse than thy old father
> Menenius does! O my son, my son! Thou art preparing
> fire for us; look thee, here's water to quench it. I was
> hardly moved to come to thee, but being assured none
> but myself could move thee, I have been blown out of
> your gates with sighs and conjure thee to pardon Rome,
> and thy petitionary countrymen. The good gods assuage
> thy wrath, and turn the dregs of it upon this varlet here;
> this, who, like a block, hath denied my access to thee.

Coriolanus
Away!

Menenius
How! away!

Coriolanus
Wife, mother, child, I know not. My affairs
Are servanted to others. Though I alone
Owe my revenge, my remission lies
In Volscian breasts. That we have been familiar,
Ingrate forgetfulness shall poison, rather
Than pity note how much. Therefore, begone.
Mine ears against your suits are stronger than
Your gates against my force. Yet, for I loved thee,
Take this along; I writ it for thy sake
And would have rent it. Another word, Menenius,
I will not hear thee speak. This man, Aufidius,
Was my beloved in Rome; yet thou behold'st!

Aufidius
You keep a constant temper.

Exeunt **Coriolanus** *and* **Aufidius**.

Menenius
He is grown from man to dragon. This Martius has wings;
he's more than a creeping thing. When he walks, he

moves like an engine, and the ground shrinks before his treading. There is no more mercy in him than there is milk in a male tiger. What he bids be done is finished with his bidding. He wants nothing of a god but eternity and a heaven to throne in.

First Sentinel

Now, sir, is your name Menenius?

Second Sentinel

'Tis a spell, you see, of much power. You know the way home again.

First Sentinel

Do you hear how we are shent for keeping your greatness back?

Second Sentinel

What cause, do you think, I have to swoon?

Menenius

I neither care for the world nor your general. For such things as you, I can scarce think there's any, you're so slight. He that hath a will to die by himself fears it not from another. Let your general do his worst. For you, be that you are, long; and your misery increase with your age! I say to you, as I was said to, Away!

Exit.

First Sentinel

A noble fellow, I warrant him.

Second Sentinel

The worthy fellow is our general. He's the rock, the oak not to be wind-shaken.

Exeunt.

5.3

Enter **Coriolanus**, **Aufidius**, *and others*.

Coriolanus
We will before the walls of Rome tomorrow
Set down our host. My partner in this action,
You must report to the Volscian lords, how plainly
I have borne this business.

Aufidius
                Only their ends
You have respected, stopped your ears against
The general suit of Rome, never admitted
A private whisper, no, not with such friends
That thought them sure of you.

Coriolanus
                   This last old friend,
Whom with a cracked heart I have sent to Rome,
Loved me above the measure of a father,
Nay, godded me, indeed. Their latest refuge
Was to send him, for whose old love I have,
Though I showed sourly to him, once more offered
The first conditions, which they did refuse
And cannot now accept, to grace him only
That thought he could do more. A very little
I have yielded to. Fresh embassies and suits,
Nor from the state nor private friends, hereafter
Will I lend ear to. Ha! What shout is this?
Shall I be tempted to infringe my vow
In the same time 'tis made? I will not.

Enter in mourning habits, **Virgilia**, **Volumnia**, *leading young*
Martius, **Valeria**, *and Attendants*.

My wife comes foremost; then the honoured mould
Wherein this trunk was framed, and in her hand
The grandchild to her blood. But, out, affection!
All bond and privilege of nature, break!
Let it be virtuous to be obstinate.

What is that curtsy worth? Or those doves' eyes,
Which can make gods forsworn? I melt, and am not
Of stronger earth than others. My mother bows,
As if Olympus to a molehill should
In supplication nod, and my young boy
Hath an aspect of intercession, which
Great nature cries 'Deny not.' Let the Volsces
Plough Rome and harrow Italy, I'll never
Be such a gosling to obey instinct, but stand,
As if a man were author of himself
And knew no other kin.

Virgilia

My lord and husband!

Coriolanus

These eyes are not the same I wore in Rome.

Virgilia

The sorrow that delivers us thus changed
Makes you think so.

Coriolanus

Like a dull actor now,
I have forgot my part, and I am out,
Even to a full disgrace. Best of my flesh,
Forgive my tyranny, but do not say
For that 'Forgive our Romans.' O, a kiss
Long as my exile, sweet as my revenge!
Now, by the jealous queen of heaven, that kiss
I carried from thee, dear; and my true lip
Hath virgined it e'er since. You gods! I prate,
And the most noble mother of the world
Leave unsaluted. Sink, my knee, i' the earth;

Kneels.

Of thy deep duty more impression show
Than that of common sons.

Volumnia

O, stand up blest!
Whilst, with no softer cushion than the flint,
I kneel before thee, and unproperly
Show duty, as mistaken all this while
Between the child and parent.

Kneels.

Coriolanus

What is this?
Your knees to me? to your corrected son?
Then let the pebbles on the hungry beach
Strike at the stars. Then let the mutinous winds
Fling the proud cedars 'gainst the fiery sun,
Murdering impossibility, to make
What cannot be, slight work.

Volumnia

Thou art my warrior;
I helped to frame thee. Do you know this lady?

Coriolanus

The noble sister of Publicola,
The moon of Rome, chaste as the icicle
That's congealed by the frost from purest snow
And hangs on Dian's temple: dear Valeria!

Volumnia

This is a poor epitome of yours,
Which by the interpretation of full time
May show like all yourself.

Coriolanus

The god of soldiers,
With the consent of supreme Jove, inform
Thy thoughts with nobleness, that thou mayst prove
To shame unvulnerable, and stick i' the wars
Like a great sea-mark, standing every flaw,
And saving those that eye thee!

Volumnia

                    Your knee, sirrah.

Coriolanus

That's my brave boy!

Volumnia

Even he, your wife, this lady, and myself,
Are suitors to you.

Coriolanus

                    I beseech you, peace;
Or, if you'd ask, remember this before:
The thing I have forsworn to grant may never
Be held by you denials. Do not bid me
Dismiss my soldiers, or capitulate
Again with Rome's mechanics. Tell me not
Wherein I seem unnatural. Desire not
To ally my rages and revenges with
Your colder reasons.

Volumnia

                    O, no more, no more!
You have said you will not grant us any thing,
For we have nothing else to ask but that
Which you deny already. Yet we will ask,
That, if you fail in our request, the blame
May hang upon your hardness: therefore hear us.

Coriolanus

Aufidius, and you Volsces, mark; for we'll
Hear nought from Rome in private. Your request?

Volumnia

Should we be silent and not speak, our raiment
And state of bodies would betray what life
We have led since thy exile. Think with thyself
How more unfortunate than all living women
Are we come hither, since that thy sight, which should
Make our eyes flow with joy, hearts dance with comforts,
Constrains them weep and shake with fear and sorrow,

Making the mother, wife and child to see
The son, the husband and the father tearing
His country's bowels out. And to poor we
Thine enmity's most capital. Thou barr'st us
Our prayers to the gods, which is a comfort
That all but we enjoy. For how can we,
Alas, how can we for our country pray.
Whereto we are bound, together with thy victory,
Whereto we are bound? Alack, or we must lose
The country, our dear nurse, or else thy person,
Our comfort in the country. We must find
An evident calamity, though we had
Our wish, which side should win. For either thou
Must, as a foreign recreant, be led
With manacles through our streets, or else
Triumphantly tread on thy country's ruin,
And bear the palm for having bravely shed
Thy wife and children's blood. For myself, son,
I purpose not to wait on fortune till
These wars determine. If I cannot persuade thee
Rather to show a noble grace to both parts
Than seek the end of one, thou shalt no sooner
March to assault thy country than to tread –
Trust to't, thou shalt not – on thy mother's womb,
That brought thee to this world.

Virgilia

Ay, and mine,
That brought you forth this boy, to keep your name
Living to time.

Young Martius

A' shall not tread on me.
I'll run away till I am bigger, but then I'll fight.

Coriolanus

Not of a woman's tenderness to be,
Requires nor child nor woman's face to see.
I have sat too long.

Rising.

Volumnia
                              Nay, go not from us thus.
If it were so that our request did tend
To save the Romans, thereby to destroy
The Volsces whom you serve, you might condemn us,
As poisonous of your honour. No, our suit
Is that you reconcile them, so the Volsces
May say 'This mercy we have show'd,' the Romans,
'This we received,' and each in either side
Give the all-hail to thee and cry 'Be blest
For making up this peace!' Thou know'st, great son,
The end of war's uncertain, but this certain,
That, if thou conquer Rome, the benefit
Which thou shalt thereby reap is such a name,
Whose repetition will be dogged with curses,
Whose chronicle thus writ: 'The man was noble,
But with his last attempt he wiped it out;
Destroyed his country, and his name remains
To the ensuing age abhorred.' Speak to me, son.
Think'st thou it honourable for a noble man
Still to remember wrongs? Daughter, speak you;
He cares not for your weeping. Speak thou, boy.
Perhaps thy childishness will move him more
Than can our reasons. There's no man in the world
More bound to 's mother; yet here he lets me prate
Like one i' the stocks. Thou hast never in thy life
Show'd thy dear mother any courtesy,
When she, poor hen, fond of no second brood,
Has clucked thee to the wars and safely home,
Loaden with honour. Say my request's unjust,
And spurn me back. But if it be not so,
Thou art not honest, and the gods will plague thee,
That thou restrain'st from me the duty which
To a mother's part belongs. He turns away.
Down, ladies; let us shame him with our knees.
To his surname Coriolanus 'longs more pride

Than pity to our prayers. Down. An end;
This is the last: so we will home to Rome,
And die among our neighbours. Nay, behold 's.
This boy, that cannot tell what he would have
But kneels and holds out hands for fellowship,
Does reason our petition with more strength
Than thou hast to deny 't. Come, let us go.
This fellow had a Volscian to his mother;
His wife is in Corioles and his child
Like him by chance. Yet give us our dispatch.
I am hushed until our city be afire,
And then I'll speak a little.

He holds her by the hand, silent.

Coriolanus
                    O mother, mother!
What have you done? Behold, the heavens do ope,
The gods look down, and this unnatural scene
They laugh at. O my mother, mother! O!
You have won a happy victory to Rome;
But, for your son – believe it, O, believe it –
Most dangerously you have with him prevail'd,
If not most mortal to him. But, let it come.
Aufidius, though I cannot make true wars,
I'll frame convenient peace. Now, good Aufidius,
Were you in my stead, would you have heard
A mother less? Or granted less, Aufidius?

Aufidius
I was moved withal.

Coriolanus
                  I dare be sworn you were.
And, sir, it is no little thing to make
Mine eyes to sweat compassion. But, good sir,
What peace you'll make, advise me. O mother! Wife!
I'll not to Rome, but by and by fear not
But we will drink together. You deserve
To have a temple built you; all the swords

In Italy, and her confederate arms,
Could not have made this peace. Farewell. Farewell.

Exeunt **Volumnia**, **Virgilia**, *etc*.

Aufidius, what peace you'll make, advise me.

Aufidius
We must proceed as we do find the people.
Go, tell the lords o'th'city what is done,
Even in theirs and the commons' ears
I will avouch the truth of it. This traitor -

Coriolanus
How now? Traitor?

Aufidius
Ay, traitor, Martius!

Coriolanus
Martius!

Aufidius
Ay, Martius, Caius Martius. Dost thou think
I'll grace thee with that robbery, thy stol'n name
Coriolanus in Corioles?
Being banished, you did come unto my hearth,
Presented to my knife your throat; I took you,
Made you joint-servant with me, gave you way
In all your own desires; nay, let you choose
Out of my files, your projects to accomplish,
My best and freshest men; till, at the last,
I seemed your follower, not partner; yet,
What faults you made before the last, I think
Might have found easy fines. But here to end
Where we were to begin, and give away
The benefit of our levies, answering us
With our own charge, making a treaty where
There was a yielding – this admits no excuse.
Volsces, He has betrayed your business, and given up,
For certain drops of salt, your city Rome –

I say 'your city' – to his wife and mother,
And at their tears, which are as cheap as lies,
He whined and roared away your victory,
That pages blushed at him and men of heart
Looked wondering each at other.

Coriolanus

                              Hear'st thou, Mars?

Aufidius

Name not the god, thou boy of tears!

Coriolanus

                              Ha!

Aufidius

No more.

Coriolanus

Measureless liar, thou hast made my heart
Too great for what contains it. Boy! O slave!
Cut me to pieces, Volsces. Men and lads,
Stain all your edges on me. Boy! false hound!
If you have writ your annals true, 'tis there,
That, like an eagle in a dove-cote, I
Fluttered your Volscians in Corioles.
Alone I did it. Boy!

Aufidus

My rage is gone,
And I am struck with sorrow. Let him die for't.
The fault is mine. I raised him, and I pawned
My honour for his truth. We patient fools,
Whose children he hath slain, our base throats tore
With giving him glory. Take him up.

Coriolanus *is slain.*

Aufidus

Hold, hold, hold, hold! Though in this city he
Hath widowed and unchilded many a one,

Which to this hour bewail the injury,
Yet he shall have a noble memory. Assist.

Exeunt, bearing the body of **Coriolanus**. *A dead march sounded.*

5.4

Enter **Volumnia**.

First Senator
Behold our patroness, the life of Rome!
Call all your tribes together, praise the gods,
And make triumphant fires. Strew flowers before them.
Unshout the noise that banish'd Martius,
Repeal him with the welcome of his mother.
Cry 'Welcome, ladies, welcome!'

Exeunt.